D1068036

Date: 11/4/21

808.8245 MON
Monologues for actors of
color : Men /

Monologues
for Actors
of Color

Monologues for Actors of Color

Men

edited by Roberta Uno

Routledge
Taylor & Francis Group

LONDON AND NEW YORK

First published 2000 by Routledge

2 Park Square, Milton Park, Abingdon, Oxon OX14 4RN
711 Third Avenue, New York, NY 10017, USA

Routledge is an imprint of the Taylor & Francis Group, an informa business

First issued in hardback 2016

Text design by Tara Klurman

Copyright and permissions acknowledgments can be found on pages 157–61 of this book. These pages shall be considered an extension of this copyright page. We have made every reasonable effort to identify and locate copyright owners. If any information is found to be incomplete, we will gladly make whatever additional permissions acknowledgments might be necessary.

Library of Congress Cataloging-in-Publication Data
Monologues for actors of color : men / edited by Roberta Uno.

    p. cm.

ISBN 0-87830-070-8.—ISBN 0-87830-071-6 (pbk.)

1. Monologues. 2. Minorities—United States Drama. 3. Men Drama.

4. American Drama—20th century. I. Uno, Roberta, 1956– .

PN2080.M535 2000

808.82'45'081—dc21   99-14179

                                            CIP

ISBN 978-0-87830-071-6 (pbk)
ISBN 978-1-138-17541-9 (hbk)

For the many fine actors who have graced the stage
at **New WORLD Theater**

Keep telling all of our stories

Contents

Preface

While working on this and a companion collection for women, an incident occurred, poignant and revealing in nature, which spoke to the need for such an actor's resource. The phone rang in the middle of the night and a young actor introduced himself asking, "Can you tell me where I can find a monologue written for a black, gay character?" Suppressing the impulse to ask him when my phone number had become an actor crisis hotline, I was intrigued by the desperation in his voice and the specificity of the question. When I questioned why he was looking for this monologue with such urgency that he had found it necessary to wake up a complete stranger, he apologized and explained that he was preparing for his final monologue assignment in four years of studying acting and, as a black gay actor, he had played a range of characters, but had never had the opportunity to inhabit the skin of a character who spoke to his most primary identities. He wondered aloud, did such material exist?

A symposium entitled "Training the Actor of Color," convened by the Tisch School of the Arts of New York University in 1994, brought this question to the foreground when actors of color in the audience spoke about their peripheral existence in major training programs. One observed that even in situations where the student is not an obvious racial minority in an acting class or a production, reading lists and course assignments typically draw from a very narrow and Eurocentric canon. Another spoke enthusiastically about her experience acting in classics of European theater, but emphasized the special joy of speaking from the stage as a black woman, embodying an image often invisible or misrepresented in American society.

The issue of racial representation on the contemporary Western stage has historically been problematic, informed as it is by societal racism, a distorted and omnipresent media, the legacy of the American minstrel show, and the power dynamics of production. Although it's been some three decades since pioneers of the practice of nontraditional casting, such as C. Bernard Jackson, Joseph Papp, and Randall "Duk" Kim, opened the European canon to interpretation by actors of all races, surprisingly many theater directors still consider the idea "new."

Ironically, for many actors of color, "nontraditional casting" would mean the opportunity to portray one's own racial identity on stage. Asian American actors are all too familiar with everyone from Marlon Brando to Katherine Hepburn to Jonathan Pryce portraying Asians; Native American actors suffer the "war-paint-and-wigs Indians" born of spaghetti westerns; and Latino actors see choice film roles consistently going to Anglo actors with household name recognition. All find themselves frequently cast as "backdrop" or "sidekick" to the story of a white protagonist in any number of settings—South Africa, Hawaii, Los Angeles, New York, the American West or South—where frequently they serve to teach that protagonist a profound lesson about humanity. Many actors share absurdly painful stories of being asked to audition "more black" or "more street" or with a thicker accent. In his unpublished solo performance piece, *Assimilation*, actor/writer Shushir Kurup portrays a South Asian actor following a casting director's instructions to become "more Indian"; the audience is mesmerized by his self-maiming transformation into a subhuman caricature that wins the unseen arbiter's approval.

This collection is intended to shift the point of focus from periphery to center, to characters who are more than setting for a "larger" story, the moral conscience of the story, or of tangential interest. My primary criteria were excellent writing, engaging acting material, and centrality of the character in the world of the play. I have chosen a range of contemporary excerpts, all from published sources because it is essential that any actor understand the context of an isolated speech. Included are samplings of works that have clearly entered the canon, by authors such as Le Roi Jones (Imamu Baraka), Frank Chin, George C. Wolfe, Wole Soyinka, and August Wilson, along with work by new, experimental, and international writers. Dramatic form includes traditional drama, as well as choreopoem, and text from solo performance, reflecting the aesthetic streams and impulses that have invigorated the contemporary theater.

A caveat: This resource is not intended to confine an actor within a box defined by gender, race, ethnicity, or national identity. I have seen, for example, both an Asian and a Caucasian actor interpret Charles Fuller's harrowing *Zooman* monologue with fascinating and different nuances and implications. What you have before you is powerful writing that promises to expand possibilities in performance and introduce a wider canon and an expanded, complex dramaturgy.

Roberta Uno
Amherst, Massachusetts

Before It Hits Home
Cheryl L. West

Act 2. The Bailey home.

Wendal is a Black male in his early 30s, a jazz saxophonist who has been hiding the fact that he has AIDS from his family and from his girlfriend. He is in denial about his bisexuality, telling his doctor, "Don't know why I'm even here. You see, I can't have AIDS. Look, I got a woman...we thinking about getting married.... I don't mess with no men...." The only person he tells is his lover, Douglass, who is also leading a secret life apart from his children and wife. As Wendal's condition rapidly declines, Douglass helps Wendal get a train ticket home. When Wendal tells his mother that he has AIDS, she demands to know how he got the disease. Finally honest with her and himself, he tells her, "I have relationships with women and sometimes with men." She exhorts him to pray: "You better get down on your knees right now boy and you better pray, beg God's forgiveness for your nasty wicked ways...."

WENDAL: Pray! Mama, what in the hell you think I've been doing? I've prayed every night. I laid in that hospital bed thirty-two days and thirty-two nights and all I did was pray. You know how lonely it is Mama to lay in a bed that ain't even your own for thirty-two days, nothing but tubes and your own shit to keep you company; what it is to bite into a pillow

1

all night so people can't hear you screaming? No TV, I didn't even have a quarter to buy myself a paper. I tried to get right with your God, I asked him for some spare time, to keep me from pitching my guts every hour, to keep me from shitting all over myself, to give me the strength to wipe my ass good enough so I didn't have to smell myself all night. I prayed that they would stop experimenting on me, stop the rashes, the infections, the sores up my ass. I prayed Mama for some company. I prayed that somebody would get their room wrong and happen into mine so I could talk to somebody, maybe they would even put their arms around me 'cause I was so damn scared, maybe it would be somebody who would come back, somebody who would want to know me for who I really was and I prayed harder and I prayed to your God that if I could just hold on, if I could just get home . . . I'm not going to apologize Mama for loving who I loved, I ain't even gonna apologize for getting this shit, I've lived a lie and I'm gonna have to answer for that, but I'll be damn if I'm gon' keep lying, I ain't got the energy. I'm a deal with it just like you taught me to deal with everything else that came my way . . . but I could use a little help Mama. . . .

Blade to the Heat
Oliver Mayer

1959. A gym.

Wilfred Vinal is a vicious boxer vying to fight for the middleweight title. The reigning champion, Mantequilla Decima, has just been beaten in an upset victory by a newcomer, Pedro Quinn. In order to get a shot at Quinn, Vinal must first fight Mantequilla, who is anxious to vindicate himself in a rematch. Vinal embarks on a blatant psychological assault on both Decima and Quinn, accusing them of being homosexuals. In the ring with Decima, Vinal taunts him: "What are you, some kinda faggot? A maricon? . . . Little nancy boy! Little Cubano bon-bon. . . ."

Furious after losing to Decima in a split decision, Vinal throws a tantrum, inciting the crowd. "He didn't beat me! He's a fag! . . . And Pete Quinn, he's the biggest fag of all!" Later, enjoying the attention of reporters, Vinal mocks the sexuality and the mixed Latino heritage of the new champion, Quinn: ". . . Little half-breed cholo bastid. . .I ain't no mixed blood. Yo soy boricua! Puro sangre. . .I better not bump into him in no men's room 'cause my papi told me don't stand for no patitos." When Jack, an ex-fighter and Quinn's trainer, confronts Vinal—"You don't SAY that, not in this line of business. You KNOW that. You tryna destroy him? . . ." —Vinal justifies his allegations.

VINAL: You come to a stinky gym like this for a reason. It's always something. Some assholes they just like to fight. Other guys they got to prove something. The little ones they got a complex. Big ones they got a complex too. Some of these clowns like to beat on other guys to impress the chicks, like it'll make their dick bigger or something. Then there's the other kind. They here 'cause they like the smell of men. They like to share sweat. They like the form, man. The way a dude looks when he throws a blow, his muscles all strained and sweaty, his ass all tight bearing down on the blow, his mouth all stopped up with a piece of rubber, and only a pair of soaking wet trunks between his johnson and yours. They like it. And they like to catch a whupping for liking it. That's just the way it is. I'm surprised, man. Thought you knew the business, old-timer.

Born in the R.S.A.
A collaborative effort by Barney Simon and the cast (Vanessa Cooke, Melanie Dobbs, Timmy Kwebulana, Neil McCarthy, Geina Mhlophe, Fiona Ramsay, Thoko Ntshinga, and Terry Norton)

Apartheid-era South Africa.

Zacharia is a black South African, an unemployed double bass musician who is a subtenant of a black trade unionist, Thenjiwe Bona. At the time he rented the room, Zacharia was aware that it contained a hidden drawer where pamphlets were stored for the African National Congress: "She opened it and says, 'I'm sorry but this comes with the room. It's the only safe place.' The drawer was full of pamphlets, I pick one up, ANC. She looks at me and says 'How do you feel now?' I said 'Shit, OK, I'll help you fold them.'"

Thenjiwe's sister's children live with her, and Zacharia takes a particular liking to ten-year-old Dumisani: "I took him to gigs with me, he had a real feel for jazz. He became a mascot, a buddy . . . I've got two kids of my own. I've never lived with either of them so I began to understand what I was missing. . . ." Thenjiwe is later abducted by the security police, who also arrest little Dumisani on a false charge of throwing stones at the police. Zacharia's life converges with those of other characters in the play who are on both sides of the apartheid system as a search for the two reveals a story of brutality and betrayal. At this point of the play Zacharia tells of

finally locating the badly beaten Dumisani, who has just been released
and is convalescing in the home of an activist white lawyer.

ZACHARIA: I went to see Dumisani at Mia's house in Saxonwold. I took
his baseball bat and his recorder. I hadn't been out of Soweto for
weeks. I heard that guy. . .talking about landing on the moon. That's
what Saxonwold felt like. Those houses, those gardens, that cool
sprinkling water. It was insanity. I sat in a bus full of domestic ser-
vants and gardeners and listened to their chatter. This was what they
saw and did and said every day. My head was buzzing. Anyway I got
off at the right stop in Oxford Road. It was near the convent school.
Her house wasn't as big as the others but the garden was beautiful. . . .

Mia answered the door herself.

Can I see him? We tiptoed down the passage and stopped at a door.
She opened it. Dumisani was lying on his back in a big double bed.
His face was swollen, his eyes closed. Everything around him was little blue flowers. The curtains. The wallpaper. The cushion under his
head. He started moaning and Mia quickly closed the door. . . .

I just wanted to pick him up and carry him home. I walked back
towards the bus stop. I realized that I was still carrying his baseball
bat and recorder. As I passed the convent school I was still thinking
of Dumisani. The playground was full of little white girls in their neat
uniforms having their morning break. I watched them running,
laughing, and playing and I thought, Ja, do you know who's watching you? Your mummy told you to be afraid of me. I thought, ja, every
one of you has a nanny. She feeds you, she comforts you, she washes

6

that uniform, she polishes those shoes, and every time she leaves Soweto or Alexandra and says goodbye to her own children, she doesn't know whether she'll see them again, alive or dead. Ja, your nanny knows where your kitchen knives are, she even knows where your daddy hides the revolver. Your mommy's nanny knew too. But how many of you do they kill? Ask her about our children, and the soldiers who shoot them dead. Ask her what she's waiting for? For us to prove that we can kill children as well as they can?

Suddenly I moved through the gates to the middle of the playground. I started to swing the baseball bat—skulls cracked—brains and baby teeth flew—I splintered arms and legs and spines. There was blood everywhere. I went on swinging left and right. I was a panther, I was a tiger, I was everything they wanted me to be. I was their black King Kong. A bell started to ring. I found myself on the pavement. The bell was calling to children to go inside. I continued to watch them play. I couldn't breathe. I turned and started to walk up Oxford Road. I heard myself yelling Fuck you! Fuck you! Fuck you for what you have done to Dumisani and fuck you fuck you fuck you for what you are doing to me.

A Bowl of Beings
Culture Clash

"Ricflections"

A Bowl of Beings is the Latino comedy troupe Culture Clash's "Valentine card to the Chicano Movement." Culture Clash, comprised of Richard Montoya, Ricardo Salinas, and Herbert Siguenza, are writers/performers who have created a body of works that use physical comedy, satire, and political commentary to explore clashing cultures in a changing American society. In this monologue, Ric relates an autobiographical story of a young comedian/actor whose career was nearly stopped by a random act of violence.

Ric: Grandfather. Hey Abuelo. I was about five when I first remember you, mí abuelo. You would take your white handkerchief, grab the tips, roll it in the air and then chase me, and at the right moment you would snap my butt. And, damn it would hurt. But you know something mí abuelo, I loved every minute of it. Papa Wenceslao. He was about seventy-two years old then. Wenceslao. How the hell did he get that name! He first married when he was fifty, my grandma was thirty. Sly, huh? He was an atheist, vegetarian, dark-complexioned Indio with silver-white hair. He always wore a suit and tie, even to picnics. And he had this gray fedora. He looked like a Latino George Raft. He died when he was ninety-three back in 1978.

Well, about a year ago I saw him again. In the hospital. I was laid out pretty bad. I felt his presence; I know he was there with me. I was in the intensive care unit for about a week. We were having a Culture Clash meeting at my house in the Mission District of San Francisco when we heard a disturbance out front. We went to check out what was happening. There was a kid getting beat up by a gang. They were beating him up real bad. I said, "Hey, he's had enough, let him go." I didn't even get in between them. Well it was dark outside, but I could see from about twelve feet away there was someone in a trench coat. He pulled out a sawed-off shotgun. I saw a flash of light, and I was shot!

It happened so fast. I got shot and I couldn't believe it. I kept shouting: "I got shot! I got shot? I got shot?" It was like a movie. But then, it became real. So real that it became larger than life. It's hard to describe how my life flashed in front of me. It was more like a feeling. I remember my life, just slipping away. Yet a feeling more intense than I've ever felt. Each breath, I thought, was my last. I felt my life leaving me slowly, gently, delicately. I remember thinking that I was going to go into a deep sleep and find out what the fuck was on the other side. I mean I was right there on the edge. Then I yelled out, "Don't tell my mother!" Could you believe that? It was like when I was a little boy and I broke that expensive vase. Don't tell my mama. Everything was so three-dimensional. My mind began to work frantically fast. It was the epitome of panic. But this is what I think saved my life. I got angry, I felt ripped off. You mean this is the way I'm gonna leave this place? This isn't the way it's supposed to be. I'm not ready to go! I mean, one minute I was planning how we were going to come to L.A. and make people laugh, (*Pause*) and the next minute some motherfucking gang member blows me away! He turned out to be seventeen years old—seventeen years old. A kid with a big gun.

To this day, I don't know why, I never felt vengeful. In a way I feel sorry for him and so many others like him. There's a bigger picture out there. But hey, talking to you is like therapy to me. Can you blame me? It's cheaper than seeing a shrink. Well, I've been going to a doctor—not even a doctor, I get to see a surgeon. And my surgeon says that I'm eighty-five percent all there. Well, last year I asked him if it was OK to get back with the guys and he said, "Whatever makes you happy." And this makes me happy. So here I am, (*Like a broken record*) eighty-five percent, eighty-five percent, eighty-five percent . . .

But you know what really made me angry that night? I had just bought a brand-new, expensive Calvin Klein shirt. That really hurt. The guys kid around with me now. Whenever I lag behind they yell, "Hey Ric, get the lead out." But I look at the bright side of things; now I can drink all the beer I want and not get drunk, 'cause when I drink beer it all pours out of me.

After I got shot I was knocked to the ground and my homeboy Richard was right above me. He said, "Ric, buddy, is there anything I could do for you?" "Rich," I said, "Call 911." He said, "OK! What's the number?" Meanwhile death is ready to dance the mambo with me, right?

I know I got a second chance on life, and I don't take life for granted. And, I know this may sound corny but what the hell . . .

Enjoy life, respect yourselves, respect your loved ones, love your neighbors, a good hug now and then. Stop the violence; it's as simple as that. Bueno pues, tómenlo suave. (*He starts to leave and then stops*)

Hey Abuelo, it was good to see you again, thanks for being there. My doctor says I'm eighty-five percent now . . . chingao. I wonder where the fifteen percent went?

"In beauty may I walk. In beauty before me may I walk. In beauty behind me may I walk. In beauty above me may I walk. And in old age, wandering in a trail of beauty, lively may I walk. And in old age, wandering in a trail of beauty, living again may I walk. It is finished in beauty. It is finished in beauty."

A Branch of the Blue Nile
Derek Walcott

Act 1. Scene 2. Late afternoon. The bare stage of a small theater in Trinidad.

Gavin Fontinelle is an actor in his early thirties who is fully committed to his calling: "I avoid emotional entanglements, I hoard myself for my work . . . I'll love you all for as long as things work out. I don't waste emotion on what's transient." His cynical detachment ebbs for a short while when he experiences the "spark" of true connection to a character embodied in another actor. Soon afterwards his cynicism returns; in this monologue he attempts to communicate how hard it is to be an actor in a world which has judged and sterotyped him by his appearance.

GAVIN: At first off, I didn't see myself in the mirror.
I just plain refused what they wanted me to see,
which was a black man looking back in my face
and muttering: "How you going han'le this, nigger?
How you going leap out of the invisible crowd
and be your charming, dazzling self?" I saw me;
then the mirror changed on me, the way you hate
your passport picture. I saw a number under it
like a prison picture, a mug shot in a post office,

13

and I began to believe what I saw in the mirror
because that's how they wanted me to look.
I reduced that reflection to acceptance, babe,
against my mother-fucking will, accept the odds,
accept the definition, accept the roles
if you wanted more than some shit-shrieking,
fist-jerking, suicidal revolutionary protest
in some back alley of the alleged Afro-American
avant-garde, so I gave in to the mirror,
I melted right into it, and I despised myself,
because I gave no trouble, and I got work.
You do the same, and you'll do fine, you'll make the top
a secondary role; the best for us is second,
I had an actor friend, black guy in New York.
He was convinced that things would change.
People, once he made it, would love each other.
Know where he is, Miss Sheila? Overdose.
Dead in the conviction that there was no justice,
no opportunity for his genius, which, being black,
was treated as presumption on his part.
He was praised for being the exception.
That's what brought me back for a while.
To walk the beach, play tennis, do a show like this
for almost nothing, and to reconsider.
Harden my heart a little, then head back.
Drive a cab, push racks up Seventh Avenue.
Remember you all. Sounds callous, eh? But
we're actors, baby. Rent out our emotions.
That means our devotion is as dependable
as a mercenary's or a hooker's. Any more?

14

The Chickencoop Chinaman
Frank Chin

Act 2, Scene 1. The Oakland district of Pittsburgh, Pennsylvania. The late sixties.

Tam Lum is "a Chinese American writer filmmaker with a gift of gab and an open mouth. A multi-tongued word magician losing his way to the spell who trips to Pittsburgh to conjure with his childhood friend, Kenji, and research a figure in his documentary movie." Tam's speech "jumps between black and white rhythms and accents"; he identifies himself as a "Chinaman": "My dear in the beginning there was the Word! Then there was me! And the Word was CHINAMAN. And there was me. . . . I lived the WORD! The WORD is my heritage. . . . For I am a Chinaman! A miracle synthetic! . . . I talk the talk of orphans. . . ." Tam's monologue at the rise of Act 2 describes his boyhood search for a Chinese American hero, the beginning of a struggle with identity, mythology, and dual realities.

TAM: Did ya hear that . . . ? Listen, children, did I ever tellya, I ever tellya the Lone Ranger ain't a Chinaman? I ever tellya that? Don't blame me. That's what happens when you're a Chinaman boy in the kitchen, listening in the kitchen to the radio, for what's happenin in the other world, while grandmaw has an ear for nothing but ancient trains in the night, and talks pure Chinamouth you understood only

15

by love and feel. She don't hear what a boy hears. She's for the Chinese Hour and chugablood red roving, livin to hear one train, once more. I heard JACK ARMSTRONG, ALL-AMERICAN BOY fight Japs, come outa the radio everyday into our kitchen to tell me everyday for years that ALL-AMERICAN BOYS are the best boys, the hee-rohs! the movie stars! that ALL-AMERICAN BOYS are white boys everyday, all their life long. And grandmaw heard thunder in the Sierra hundreds of miles away and listened for the Chinaman-known Iron Moonhunter, that train built by Chinamans who knew they'd never be given passes to ride the rails they laid. So of all American railroaders, only they sung no songs, told no jokes, drank no toasts to the ol' iron horse, but stole themselves some iron on the way, slowly stole up a pile of steel, children, and hid there in the granite face of the Sierra and builded themselves a wild engine to take them home. Every night, children, grandmaw listened in the kitchen, waiting, til the day she died. And I'd spin the dial looking for to hear ANYBODY, CHINESE AMERICAN BOY, ANYBODY, CHINESE AMERICAN BOY anywhere on the dial, doing anything grand on the air, anything at all. . . . I heard of the masked man. And I listened to him. And in the Sunday funnies he had black hair, and Chinatown was nothin but black hair, and for years, listen, years! I grew blind looking hard through the holes of his funnypaper mask for slanty eyes. Slanty eyes, boys! You see, I knew, children, I knew with all my heart's insight . . . shhh, listen, children . . . he wore that mask to hide his Asian eyes! And that made sense to me. I knew he wore a red shirt for good luck. I knew he rode a white horse named Silver cuz white be our color of death. Ha ha ha. And he was lucky Chinaman vengeance on the West . . . and silver bullets cuz death from a Chinaman is always expensive. Always classy. Always famous. I knew the Lone Ranger was the CHINESE AMERICAN BOY of the radio I'd looked for.

Cleveland Raining
Sung Rno

Scene 4. The Kim family house in Ohio, about a hundred miles south of Cleveland. An apocalyptic time.

Jimmy "Rodin" Kim, a Korean American man in his late twenties. "A failed artist . . . [who] walks with a noticeable limp," Jimmy has been having visions of the end of the world and devising his means to survive it: ". . . a big flood is about to come and no one seems to be aware of it. . . . For a whole year I've been dreaming about the same thing, this Volkswagen . . . in these dreams I'm floating . . . and it's raining and raining . . . Ohio becomes one big lake. . . ." His younger sister Mari—"a medical student in her early twenties. A healer"—is annoyed by his fixation on the impending flood and the fact that he has just been fired from his job as a stock boy at a supermarket. "I bet you expect me to bring in the money. . . . It's always an escape for you. . . . Why do you keep talking about this flood?" She is concerned with the disappearance of their father, who has been missing for nearly a week. The two siblings have been left on their own; their mother, a painter, abandoned them when they were small children. Mari observes, "We're a family of leavers, aren't we? We leave Korea. Then we leave each other." In this monologue, Jimmy speaks about the mysterious "hunting accident" that has left him crippled.

JIMMY: Didn't always get these things in my head. Used to follow the rules. Listened to my father, did most of what he said. He gave me

17

medical books to read. We got along fine. Then I decided to take up hunting. I went out on a day when it was wet. The sky grey, almost black. I kept walking even though I was getting lost. The rain starts coming down. It rolls down my face and it feels like I'm crying. Then I am crying. I can't really tell. It's all mixed together. I lean against a tree and I look up and this is crazy, there's this huge pencil in the sky. It's huge, monstrous. Big and yellow, the size of a tree. It's coming straight towards me, the eraser side down. Like it wants to rub me out. I said, this fucking pencil is not going to get me and I point my gun at it, only it's slippery and I feel it slipping. I hear it go off. I'm standing in a puddle. I look down and the rain is red. I'm not crying anymore. My foot's sinking deeper and deeper into this puddle. Can't move. Can't think. The rain comes down harder. I try to yell out. I can't hear myself. I'm drowned out by the wind. And I'm just this tree in a storm, the bark all stripped away. Just a naked piece of wood.

That's when I changed my name from Kim to Rodin. Kim means gold in Korean, but doesn't mean a damn thing in English. It's abstract, a word like "algebra" or "mutation." I wanted a name that meant something to me. Now Rodin was perfect, I thought. Jimmy R. Had a gangster ring to it. Someone who lived by his wits. And I had a battle wound to back it up. No one was going to mess with me.

Cloud Tectonics
José Rivera

Echo Park, Los Angeles. "Aníbal's house, a modest pre–World War II wooden bungalow, working-class, not Hollywood."

Aníbal de la Luna, "a pleasant-looking man, thirties, dressed in an American Airlines ground crew uniform," encounters Celestina del Sol at a bus stop during a rain storm. She is "soaking wet. . . . It's impossible to tell her actual age. . . . She's very, very pregnant." When he takes her home, the digital clocks on all the appliances stop; throughout the evening Celestina experiences labor pains. Aníbal tries to ascertain who she is and she tells him, "What if there are people born who don't have that sense? Don't have that inner clock telling them when a moment has passed, when another has started. . . . I'm a fifty-four-year-old woman, Aníbal, and I've been pregnant with this baby for two years. . . ." Aníbal's brother, Nelson, arrives and falls in love with Celestina even though she's pregnant with an unknown man's baby. He leaves, and Aníbal and Celestina share a meal. He makes up the sofa bed for her while she changes into her nightgown, and she returns looking "more unearthly, more angelic than ever." He tells her about his current girlfriend, Debbie, and his past loves.

ANÍBAL: I made love with Debbie just last night. Or was it this morning? (*Beat*) I had to talk her into spending the night, instead of sleeping in her office again. It seems like a million years ago. (*Beat*) I know Debbie from high school in the Bronx. We went out. Then she went out of state for college and I couldn't afford college so I stayed behind and worked. She married her English professor and moved to Ohio. I wanted to kill myself. I spent the next five years getting into these other relationships. The first one, I was twenty-two. The woman I fell in love with was thirty-nine. We had a great time together. But I took her home to meet my parents and my father made a pass at her and it was over. Then I fell in love with a blonde. She was a real beauty. But she came from this fucked-up home and she had a drug problem and she drank too much and the night I told her I didn't love her anymore she tried to throw herself out of a moving car on the Belt Parkway. Then I fell in love with a series of lesbians. Every woman I liked turned out to be gay! Then one night, New Year's Eve, I'm living in the Lower East Side, the phone rings, it's Debbie. She left her husband. She left Ohio. She was staying at her sister's in Harlem. Would I like to get together. (*Beat*) I went to her place. I didn't know what to expect. She was staying in one of those worn-out tenements with the steam heat up too high and the steel radiators that clamored all night, and Willie Colón and laughing and partying and loud kissing coming at you from all the apartments all over us. People just exploding! Going nuts! I remember the smell of *tos— tos—Tostones!* And rice and beans and *lechón—lechón—Lechón asado!* You know: everything cooked with a lot of *man—Manteca!* And I held Debbie all night long. We didn't fuck. I kissed her a lot. We touched all over. But we didn't go to bed. We were starting over. I was figuring out this new body. She seemed richer. All the years we hadn't seen each other, miles she's traveled, all this married wisdom and experience she had that I didn't have. I felt like a *boy*, a child, in the arms of this mature *woman*. We decided that night to go to Los Angeles together and start over. Be in that one city where you can really remake yourself. Pan for gold in the L.A. River. She wanted to get rich on the movies. I wanted to get away from the racists who thought of me only as a spik. (*Beat*)

As we were holding each other, touching each other, I started to remember something I thought I had forgotten. It was when I was a little boy. I don't even remember how old. We were living in Newark, New Jersey. We were visiting my cousins who lived in a big house in Patchogue, Long Island. My child's memory makes that house enormous, like a Victorian haunted house, but maybe it wasn't. They had thirteen kids. We used to watch *lucha libre* together, professional wrestling, all the time. One time my cousin Ernesto got carried away watching Bruno San Martino on TV and he punched me in the stomach. Ernie liked to inflict pain. He had long, black curly hair and a thin black mustache, freckles, large, red lips, crooked teeth: he was the cousin that looked most like me. Another night, after a party, my cousin Cheo told me how he could feel his balls flapping around in his pants when he danced to American music. His balls went flap-flap-flap when he danced to rock 'n' roll. I liked Cheo. He never punched me like Ernesto did. Cheo taught me about exponents and square roots. He went to Vietnam. Everybody thought Ernesto would get into drug dealing. (*Beat*)

One night I was on the second floor of my cousins' house. I remember walking past a dark bedroom: the door was open. I thought I heard a voice inside calling my name. I went in. My cousin Eva was there. She was older than Ernie or Cheo. Much older than me. I remember her standing by the window. I could see her face lit up by a streetlight—or was it the moon? I remember there was a heavy smell in the room. And I don't know how I eventually got there. . .but I ended up lying in bed with Eva. I was on my back, looking at the ceiling. Eva was kneeling next to me. Then Eva lifted her dress and she was straddling me and pressing her pelvis into me. I think she had her underwear on. I had my pants on and I didn't know why she was doing this to me, though I knew I had to do this because she was my older cousin, therefore she had authority. I remember her legs being smooth. I remember her face. She was looking out the window. I don't remember how long this lasted. I don't remember if anyone came in. I don't remember if anyone ever knew about this, though, later on it seemed that everybody knew. I liked Eva on top of me. I remember her weight. I liked her weight. I don't remember if I got hard or not: I was only a little boy! I liked watching Eva's face, the way she looked out the window. How the light struck half her face. I wish I could remember her mouth! I think it was open. But I don't remember. Was there a smile? Did she bite her lower lip? Was she talking to me? Did she say something in Spanish? I remember her eyes. (*Beat*)

So I fell in love with Eva. She was all I thought about. And I think my mother suspected something and she was worried about us, though first cousins had married several times in my family. One night my mother and I were washing dishes together, side by side. And we had the only conversation about sex we were ever to have. Without looking at me, she said: "Aníbal, remember: there is some fruit you are not allowed to eat." And that's all she said. And I knew exactly what she meant. And it was all she had to say to me. (*Beat*)

I've never forgotten Eva. Even in Debbie's arms after five years of missing her and wanting her, I thought easily of Eva. It's like . . . the space around my body was permanently curved—or dented—by Eva's heaviness. I wonder if love sometimes does that to you. It alters the physics around you in some way: changing the speed of light and the shape of space and how you experience time.

Cloud Tectonics
José Rivera

Epilogue. Echo Park, Los Angeles. A floating bed.

In the epilogue, forty years later, Aníbal is an old man in his seventies. Celestina enters and is "no longer pregnant. Her clothes are nicer than before. But otherwise she looks the same. She's pushing a stroller . . . she's talking to the baby. Aníbal doesn't remember her. Disappointed she reintroduces herself, prods his memory, and he begins to remember. "When he talks, he sounds like a young man again."

ANÍBAL: I searched Los Angeles for days and days after she left me. I went to that bus stop on the corner of Virgil and Santa Monica and waited there day and night. I called every hospital and went to every police station in L.A. County. (*Beat*) I imagined finding her. Living with her forever. I imagined long moments of silence between us when we didn't have anything to say. I imagined enduring the terror of a Los Angeles gone out of control because these quiet moments would be like iron wings and we'd be sheltered inside them. We wouldn't hear the noise of the earthquakes or the screams of a dying culture. But she never came back to me. I never saw her again. All I kept were memories of that extraordinary woman and a night that had that dream feeling to it, you know that feeling: there's a sound like suspended music, air that doesn't move, time that doesn't add to itself. It took me years but I finally understood that I had encountered a true mystery that night, that I had taken a living miracle into my house. That Celestina del Sol was from a world I would never understand. That sometimes Nature improvises. That Nature created a woman that lived outside the field of time and may never die. That someday everyone who ever knew her and remembered her would be gone. That she would live forever in that physical perfection like some kind of exiled and forgotten goddess. And that trying to understand such a life, and why love matters to it, why a god would need to be loved too, was like trying to understand the anatomy of the wind or the architecture of silence or cloud tectonics. (*He laughs*) Yeah. What better way to respond to a miracle than to fall in love with it?

The Colored Museum
George C. Wolfe

Soldier with a Secret

The Colored Museum is a series of exhibits in "a museum where the myths and madness of black/Negro/colored Americans are stored." In this exhibit, Junie Robinson, a black combat soldier, "comes to life and smiles at the audience. Somewhat dim-witted, he has an easygoing charm about him."

JUNIE: Pst. Pst. Guess what? I know the secret. The secret to your pain. 'Course, I didn't always know. First I had to die, then come back to life, 'fore I had the gift.

Ya see, the Cappin sent me off up ahead to scout for screamin' yella bastards. 'Course, for the life of me I couldn't understand why they'd be screamin', seein' as how we was tryin' to kill them and they us.

But anyway, I'm off lookin', when all of a sudden I find myself caught smack dead in the middle of this explosion. This blindin', burnin', scaldin' explosion. Musta been a booby trap or something, 'cause all around me is fire. Hell, I'm on fire. Like a piece of chicken dropped in a skillet of cracklin' grease. Why, my flesh was justa peelin' off of my bones.

But then I says to myself, "Junie, if yo' flesh is on fire, how come you don't feel no pain!" And I didn't. I swear as I'm standin' here, I felt nuthin'. That's when I sort of put two and two together and realized I didn't feel no whole lot of hurtin' 'cause I done died.

Well, I just picked myself up and walked right on out of that explosion. Hell, once you know you dead, why keep on dyin', ya know?

So, like I say, I walk right outta that explosion, fully expectin' to see white clouds, Jesus, and my mama, only all I saw was more war. Shootin' goin' on way off in this direction and that direction. And there, standin' around, was all the guys. Hubert, J. F., the Cappin. I guess the sound of the explosion must of attracted 'em, and they all starin' at me like I'm some kind of ghost.

So I yells to 'em, "Hey there, Hubert! Hey there, Cappin!" But they just stare. So I tells 'em how I'd died and how I guess it wasn't my time 'cause here I am, "fully in the flesh and not a scratch to my bones." And they still just stare. So I took to starin' back.

(*The expression on* Junie's *face slowly turns to horror and disbelief.*)

Only what I saw . . . well, I can't exactly to this day describe it. But I swear, as sure as they was wearin' green and holdin' guns, they was each wearin' a piece of the future on their faces.

Yeah. All the hurt that was gonna get done to them and they was gonna do to folks was right there clear as day.

I saw how J. F., once he got back to Chicago, was gonna get shot dead by this po-lice, and I saw how Hubert was gonna start beatin' up on his old lady, which I didn't understand 'cause all he could do was talk on and on about how much he loved her. Each and every one of 'em had pain in his future and blood on his path. And God or the Devil one spoke to me and said, "Junie, these colored boys ain't gonna be the same after this war. They ain't gonna have no kind of happiness."

Well, right then and there it comes to me. The secret to their pain.

Late that night, after the medics done checked me over and found me fit for fightin', after everybody done settle down for the night, I sneaked over to where Hubert was sleepin', and with a needle I stole from the medics . . . pst, pst . . . I shot a little air into his veins. The second he died, all the hurtin'-to-come just left his face.

Two weeks later I got J. F. and after that Woodrow . . . Jimmy Joe . . . I even spent all night waitin' by the latrine 'cause I knew the Cappin always made a late-night visit and . . . pst, pst . . . I got him.

(*Smiling, quite proud of himself.*) That's how come I died and come back to life. 'Cause just like Jesus went around healin' the sick, I'm supposed to go around healin' the hurtin' all these colored boys wearin' from the war.

Pst, pst. I know the secret. The secret to your pain. The secret to yours, and yours. Pst. Pst. Pst. Pst.

(*The lights slowly fade.*)

Coyote City
Daniel David Moses

Act 1. Scene 1. Darkness.

Johnny is "a young Indian man, a ghost." In this opening scene of *Coyote City*, we see him in a flashback moments before his death in the Silver Dollar, a run-down bar in an unnamed city in Canada. Lena, "a young Indian woman" recently recovered from a nervous breakdown, has been startled out of her sleep by a phone call from Johnny, who has been dead for six months. Known for his gift of storytelling, drinking, and wild ways, he implores her, "Oh Lena, babe, don't you recognize me? . . . I'm not drunk, babe. You know me . . . I miss you . . . That time down by the river . . Your sweat was so sweet, babe. Better than wine. . . ." Still deeply in love with him, Lena promises to meet him the next night in the Silver Dollar.

JOHNNY: Give me a drink. I need a drink. Shit. I'm over here you bugger. I'm almost empty here. Come on and dispense with the booze.

Please man, I'm good for it. You can trust me. I'll pay you tomorrow first thing. Come on. Come on, man, really.

Hey you want my knife? It's a real beaut. Look at all the things, man, the gadgets. Hey, you can even cut your toenails. Come on, guy, just one more beer. Shit.

Hey, how about a date with a real doll? Shit man, she's fresh from the bush. I'll give you her number. Real pretty Indian chick. What do you say? What do you say?

How about a story my Grandad gave me? A real good story, man. A love story. Come on, man, the ladies really love to hear this story. Shit it gets them all loose. You like loose ladies, don't you? Just another beer, man, just one. That's all.

(*To the darkness*) Acting like I'm not here, like he can't see me. Acting like I'm just another drunk Indian. Think he thinks I've had enough? Do you think that too? Do you think I've had enough? Enough. Shit. You think I've had too much. Well, who the fuck are you anyway? I don't know you. I don't know you. Shit you're not even real. I know I need a drink when I meet you. I look at you and I need a drink. Hey you're nothing but a bunch of spooks. That's why I got the shakes. You're the ones took Coyote in when he was looking for his woman. But no way you're tricking me. No way. I'm too smart for you. You can't get away with all that stuper-shitting with me. You're not going to get away with anything with me. You're going to buy me a drink. Shit ya, you're going to buy me a fucking drink.

The Crossroads
Joue Kossi Efoni

A crossroads. Night.

Poet, a self-described "foreigner . . . traveling musician and dreamer," is caught at the intersection of art and politics. He "has saved his old dreams by hiding them in poems, by changing them into music." His attempts to express himself make him an outlaw and a fugitive in the eyes of those whose "only script . . . is the law."

He has been drawn to the crossroads by his love for the unnamed Woman who meets him there. Their conversation is hurried; they are conscious that their time together could be interrupted at any moment by the Cop who is pursuing Poet. Poet's monologue begins just after the Cop has been distracted from his pursuit by the Woman and Poet is left onstage alone.

Poet: Suspect. Suspect. There's that word again. As far back as I can remember, it's the same old story. Nostrils flaring like a bulldog smelling bad meat. Suspect. Like my friend the painter. He was classified suspect too. Because he used to draw pictures that people didn't always understand. So the cops would raid his place from time to time. They would tear up his books and notes and slash his paintings. Since they never found anything there, they started searching inside him, cutting him into little pieces. We'd see the painter after that, busy gluing himself back together, remolding, replastering his body. I was a child. I watched. He said it was to intimidate him they'd done that. I asked him, "Sir, what does intimidate mean?" One day he came back and discovered that among the pieces he'd gathered and started gluing together, he couldn't find his tongue. And that was it. He'll never say another word. Not a single word. He can only smile. He's the one who taught me how to smile and even to laugh, laugh about anything, about myself, my mistakes, my misfortunes. He taught me how to smile. He said that only real smiles count. A smile doesn't lie. You can't smile cynically or cruelly. That's just a grimace, nothing more. You roll up your lips like you roll up your sleeves to start beating somebody. No one is fooled. He taught me to see too. He had eyes made to see. The enormous eyes of a poet, big as oceans. And full of things. And cloudy. When they looked at you, you felt transparent. He taught me to see through opaque and closed surfaces, to turn things inside out. They didn't like his eyes here. They found them suspect. They said his eyes were gadgets for spying, hidden cameras, witch's eyes, the eyes of a clairvoyant, of a voyeur. So it goes. He smiled because he didn't realize they would tear his eyes out . . .

Cuba and His Teddy Bear
Reinaldo Povod

Act 2. A tenement apartment on the Lower East Side of Manhattan. September. The present.

The play takes place in the apartment of Cuba, a coke dealer who is trying to sell two pounds of marijuana for a friend. His son, Teddy, an aspiring writer, suggests he make the deal with an acquaintance of his, a writer he admires named Che. Che is an acclaimed writer and a heroin addict, a self-educated savant who won a Tony award. He ". . . wrote that play in the hospital, when he was in the hospital kicking that shit."

When Che arrives, there is immediate tension between him and Cuba, who is jealous and wary of his influence on Teddy. Che casually suggests Teddy accompany him to audition for a movie. Cuba reacts with suspicion and then anger upon learning the role will be that of a junkie or a mugger. Teddy turns on his father, "How 'bout if I play a drug dealer, is that better?" As Cuba and Che glare at each other, Che, "with all sincerity trying to enlighten Cuba," addresses him. "Cuba, you as a dealer, and me as a junkie, we can't live a deeper truth?" When the puzzled Cuba asks, "What truth?" Che explains:

CHE: We only exist tragically on *Baretta* and *Kojak* reruns. You, Cuba—yer a father, you gotta son, you know, yer doing what you can

33

to raise him—to a lot of people yer nothing but a drug dealer. A nasty cliche. I'm a junkie who steals. I'm a junkie who steals, like a lot of junkies do. But I'm also a junkie who steals with a Tony Award. I'm a junkie who steals, I gotta Tony Award, and I got compassion in my heart for you. (*To* JACKIE) For you. (*To* TEDDY) And for you. I'm a junkie, I steal, I gotta Tony Award—compassion—and I'm Hispanic . . . that ain't a cliche. The attitude for a junkie like me who is Spanish, is: "Turn him upside down and he got hemorrhoids." It only affects him, and his own kind, and Kojak. I'm a junkie who steals but I got compassion in my heart for the dealer who sells me my dope. (*Looks at* CUBA *intently.*) You and I deserve our space. Our time on the air.

Day of Absence
Douglas Turner Ward

The Mayor's Office. An unnamed Southern town.

This satirical fantasy is "a reverse minstrel show done in white-face" by black actors who are "urged to go for broke, yet cautioned not to ham it up too broadly. In fact—it just might be more effective if they aspire for serious tragedy. Only qualification needed for Caucasian casting is that the company fit a uniform pattern—insipid white; also played in white-face." The play opens "on a somnolent cracker morning—meaning no matter the early temperature, it's gonna get hot . . ." to the slow discovery that all the town's black inhabitants have disappeared overnight. As the day progresses, chaos begins to grip the town as white women are left to care for children they have never looked after, industry is paralyzed without black labor, and blacks who have been passing as whites disappear. A courier informs the Mayor that even the Mayor's brother-in-law is missing, along with "dozens of more prominent citizens—two City Council members, the chairman of the Junior Chamber of Commerce, our City College All-Southern half-back, the chair lady of the Daughters of the Confederate Rebellion, Miss Cotton-Sack Festival of the Year. . . . Dangerous evidence points to the conclusion that they have been infiltrating. . . . Secret Nigras all the while!" In a grave, impassioned, and increasingly desperate speech, the Mayor goes on national television to make an appeal to the town's absent black citizens.

35

Good evening. . . . Despite the fact that millions of you wonderful people throughout the nation are viewing and listening to this momentous broadcast—and I thank you for your concern and sympathy in this hour of our peril—I primarily want to concentrate my attention and address these remarks solely for the benefit of our departed Nigra friends who may be listening somewheres in our far-flung land to the sound of my voice. . . . If you are—it is with heart-felt emotion and fond memories of our happy association that I ask—"Where are you. . . ?" Your absence has left a void in the bosom of every single man, woman and child of our great city. I tell you—you don't know what it means for us to wake up in the morning and discover that your cheerful, grinning, happy-go-lucky faces are missing! . . . From the depths of my heart, I can only meekly, humbly suggest what it means to me personally. . . . You see—the one face I will never be able to erase from my memory is the face—not of my Ma, not of Pa, neither wife or child—but the image of the first woman I came to love so well when just a wee lad—the vision of the first human I laid clear sight on at childbirth—the profile—better yet, the full face of my dear old. . . Jemimah—God rest her soul. . . . Yes! My dear ole mammy, wit' her round ebony moonbeam gleaming down upon me in the crib, teeth shining, blood-red bandana standing starched, peaked and proud, gazing down upon me affectionately as she crooned me a Southern lullaby. . . . OH! It's a memorable picture I will eternally cherish in permanent treasure chambers of my heart, now and forever always. . . . Well, if this radiant image can remain so infinitely vivid to me all these many years after her unfortunate demise in the po' folks home—THINK of the misery the rest of us must be suffering after being freshly denied your soothing presence?! We need ya. If you kin hear me, just contact this station 'n' I will welcome you back personally. Let me just tell you that since you eloped, nothing has been the same. How could it? You're part of us, you belong to us. Just give us a sign and we'll be contented that all is well. . . . Now if you've skipped away on a little fun-fest, we understand, ha, ha. We know you like a good time and we don't begrudge it to ya. Hell—er, er, we like a good time ourselves—who doesn't? . . . In fact, think of all the good times we've had together, huh? We've had some real fun, you and us, yesiree! . . . Nobody knows better than you and I what fun we've had together. You singing us those old Southern coon songs and dancing those Nigra jigs and us clapping, prodding, 'n' spurring you on! Lots of fun, huh?! . . . OH BOY! The times we've had together. . . . If you've snucked away for a bit of fun by yourself, we'll go 'long wit' ya—long as you let us know where you at so we won't be worried about you. . . . We'll go 'long wit' you long as you don't take the joke too far. I'll admit a joke is a joke and you've played a LULU! . . . I'm warning you, we can't stand much more horsing 'round from you! Business is business 'n' fun is fun! You've had your fun so now let's get down to business! Come on back, YOU HEAR ME!!! . . . If you been hoodwinked by agents of some foreign government, I've been authorized by the President of these United States to inform you that this liberty-loving Republic is prepared to rescue you from their clutches. Don't pay no 'tention to their sireen songs and atheistic promises! You better off under our control and you know it! . . . If you been bamboozled by rabble-rousing nonsense of your own so-called leaders, we prepared to offer same protection. Just call us up! Just give us a sign! . . . Come on, give us a sign . . . give us a sign—even a teeny-weeny one. . . ??!!

(*Glances around checking on possible communications. A bevy of headshakes indicate no success.* Mayor *returns to address with desperate fervor.*)

Now look—you don't know what you doing! If you persist in this disobedience, you know all too well the consequences! We'll track you to the end of the earth, beyond the galaxy, across the stars! We'll capture you and chastise you with all the vengeance we command!

'N' you know only too well how stern we kin be when double-crossed! The city, the state, and the entire nation will crucify you for this unpardonable defiance!
(*Checks again.*)

No call. . . ? No sign. . . ? Time is running out! Deadline slipping past! They gotta respond! They gotta!
(*Resuming.*)
Listen to me! I'm begging y'all, you've gotta come back. . . ! LOOK, GEORGE!
(*Waves dirty rag aloft.*)
I brought the rag you wax the car wit'. . . . Don't this bring back memories, George, of all the days you spent shining that automobile to shimmering perfection. . . ? And you, Rufus?! . . . Here's the shoe polisher and the brush! . . . 'Member, Rufus? . . . Remember the happy mornings you spent popping this rag and whisking this brush so furiously 'till it created music that was sympho-nee to the ear. . . ? And you—MANDY? . . . Here's the waste-basket you didn't dump this morning. I saved it just for you! . . . LOOK, all y'all out there. . . ?

Don't these things mean anything to y'all? By God! Are your memories so short?! Is there nothing sacred to ya? . . . Please come back, for my sake, please! All of you—even you questionable ones! I promise no harm will be done to you! Revenge is disallowed! We'll forgive everything! Just come on back and I'll git down on my knees—
(*Immediately drops to knees.*)
I'll be kneeling in the middle of Dixie Avenue to kiss the first shoe of the first one 'a you to show up. . . . *I'll smooch any other spot you request.* . . . Erase this nightmare 'n' we'll concede any demand you make, just come on back—please???!! . . . PLEEEEEEEEZE?!!!

They wouldn't answer . . . they wouldn't answer . . .

Death and the Maiden
Ariel Dorfman

Act 3. Scene 1. The terrace of a beach house. The present. Just before evening.

Roberto Miranda, is a doctor of about fifty years, living in "a country that is probably Chile but could be any country that has given itself a democratic government after a long period of dictatorship." A Good Samaritan, he gives a ride to a lawyer, Gerardo Escobar, whose car has broken down by the side of the road. Escobar has just been selected by the country's president to head a commission which will investigate crimes of the old regime; his wife, Paulina Salas, was a victim of torture and rape under that regime. When Roberto drops Gerardo off at the couple's beach house, Paulina recognizes his voice as the doctor who supervised her torture and raped her fifteen years before. She manages to overcome him and binds his hands and feet, persuading her husband to hear her case. Claiming innocence and pleading with Escobar to control his "mad wife," Miranda finally makes his taped confession.

ROBERTO'S VOICE: I would put on the music because it helped me in my role, the role of good guy, as they call it, I would put on Schubert because it was a way of gaining the prisoners' trust. But I also knew it was a way of alleviating their suffering. You've got to believe it was a way of alleviating the prisoners' suffering. Not only the music, but everything else I did. That's how they approached me, at first.

(The lights go up as if the moon were coming out. It is nighttime. ROBERTO is in front of the cassette recorder, confessing. The Schubert fades.)

The prisoners were dying on them, they told me, they needed someone to help care for them, someone they could trust. I've got a brother, who was a member of the secret services. You can pay the communists back for what they did to Dad, he told me one night—my father had a heart attack the day the peasants took over his land at Las Toltecas. The stroke paralyzed him—he lost his capacity for speech, would spend hours simply looking at me, his eyes said, Do something. But that's not why I accepted. The real real truth, it was for humanitarian reasons. We're at war, I thought, they want to kill me and my family, they want to install a totalitarian dictatorship, but even so, they still have the right to some form of medical attention. It was slowly, almost without realizing how, that I became involved in more delicate operations, they let me sit in on sessions where my role was to determine if the prisoners could take that much torture, that much electric current. At first I told myself that it was a way of saving people's lives, and I did, because many times I told them— without it being true, simply to help the person who was being tortured—I ordered them to stop or the prisoner would die. But afterwards I began to—bit by bit, the virtue I was feeling turned into excitement—the mask of virtue fell off it and it, the excitement, it hid, it hid, it hid from me what I was doing, the swamp of what—By the time Paulina Salas was brought in it was already too late. Too late.

(The lights start to slowly go down.)

ROBERTO: . . . too late. A kind of—brutalization took over my life, I began to really truly like what I was doing. It became a game. My curiosity was partly morbid, partly scientific. How much can this woman take? More than the other one? How's her sex? Does her sex dry up when you put the current through her? Can she have an orgasm under those circumstances? She is entirely in your power, you can carry out all your fantasies, you can do what you want with her.

(*The lights continue to fade while Roberto's voice speaks on in the semidarkness, a beam of moonlight on the cassette recorder.*)

Everything they have forbidden you since ever, whatever your mother ever urgently whispered you were never to do. You begin to dream with her, with all those women. Come on, Doctor, they would say to me, you're not going to refuse free meat, are you, one of them would sort of taunt me. His name was—they called him Stud—a nickname, because I never found out his real name. They like it, Doctor, Stud would say to me—all these bitches like it and if you put on that sweet little music of yours, they'll get even cozier. He would say this in front of the women, in front of Paulina Salas he would say it, and finally I, finally I—but not one ever died on me, not one of the women, not one of the men.

(*The lights go up and it is now dawning. Roberto, untied, writes on a sheet of paper his own words from the cassette recorder. In front of him, many sheets of handwritten pages. Paulina and Gerardo watch him.*)

ROBERTO'S VOICE (*from the recorder*): As far as I can remember, I took part in the—interrogation of ninety-four prisoners, including Paulina Salas. It is all I can say. I ask forgiveness.

Dry Lips Oughta Move to Kapuskasing
Tomson Highway

Act 1. The Wasaychigan Hill Indian Reserve, Manitoulin Island. Ontario. Saturday, February 3, 1990.

Big Joey and his sidekick Creature Nataways, both thirty-nine, have just arrived at Big Joey's house with a case of beer. They discover Big Joey's wife, Gazelle Nataways, gone and Zachary Keechigeesik sprawled nude over the living room sofa, with lipstick marks on his naked bum. After taking a Polaroid, hiding his shorts, and kicking him out of the house, Creature struts like a cock, turning to Big Joey. "Zachary Jeremiah Keechigeesik never shoulda come in your house, Big Joey. Thank god, Gazelle Nataways ain't my wife no more. . . ."

As Big Joey throws him an intimidating glance, ignoring him for a hockey game on television, Creature "reverts back to his usual nervous self" and reviews Gazelle Nataways's role in their lives and friendship.

CREATURE: (*As he proceeds to try to clean up the mess around the couch, mostly shoving everything back under it.*)
I don't mind, Big Joey, I really don't. I tole you once I tole you twice she's yours now. It's like I loaned her to you, I don't mind. I can take it. We made a deal, remember? The night she threw the toaster at me and just about broke my skull, she tole me: "I had enough,

43

Creature Nataways, I had enough from you. I had your kids and I had your disease and that's all I ever want from you, I'm leavin'." And then she grabbed her suitcase and she grabbed the kids, no, she didn't even grab the kids, she grabbed the TV and she just sashayed herself over here. She left me. It's been four years now, Big Joey, I know, I know. Oh, it was hell, it was hell at first but you and me we're buddies since we're babies, right? So I thought it over for about a year . . . then one day I swallowed my pride and I got up off that chesterfield and I walked over here, I opened your door and I shook your hand and I said: "It's okay, Big Joey, it's okay." And then we went and played darts in Espanola except we kinda got side-tracked, remember?? Big Joey, we ended up on that three-day bender?

Dry Lips Oughta Move to Kapuskasing
Tomson Highway

> Act 1. The Wasaychigan Hill Indian Reserve, Manitoulin Island. Ontario. Saturday, February 3, 1990.

> Momentarily, Pierre St. Pierre, age fifty-three, arrives with the big news that he's just been made referee for the Wasy Waileretts, the new Indian women's hockey team who in a few days play their first game with the Canoe Lake Bravettes. Gazelle Nataways has booked the ice time and Pierre's wife has cleaned out his wallet and left with the other women: "Piled theirselves into seven cars and just took off. . . . Shoppin'. Hockey equipment." Big Joey and Creature listen in stunned disbelief as Pierre describes the formation of the Wasy Wailerettes.

PIERRE: Dominique Ladouche, Black Lady Halked, that terrible Dictionary woman, Fluffy Sainte-Marie, Dry Lips Manigitogan, Leonarda Lee Starblanket, Annie Cook, June Bug McLeod, Big Bum Pegahmagahbow, all twenty-seven of 'em. Them women from right here on this reserve, a whole batch of 'em, they upped and they said: "Bullshit! Ain't nobody on the face of this earth's gonna tell us us women's got no business playin' hockey. That's bullshit!" That's what they said: "Bullshit!" So. They took matter into their own hands. And, holy shit la marde, I almost forgot to tell you my wife Veronique

St. Pierre, she went and made up her mind she's joinin' the Wasy Wailerettes, only the other women wouldn't let her at first on account she never had no babies—cuz, you see, you gotta be pregnant or have piles and piles of babies to be a Wasy Wailerette—but my wife, she put her foot down and she says: "Zhaboonigan Peterson may be just my adopted daughter and she may be retarded as a doormat but she's still my baby." That's what she says to 'em. And she's on and they're playin' hockey and the Wasy Wailerettes, they're just a-rarin' to go, who woulda thunk it, huh?

Dutchman
LeRoi Jones (Imamu Baraka)

> Scene 2. "In the flying underbelly of the city. Steaming hot, and summer on top, outside. Underground. The subway heaped on modern myth."

> Clay, a "twenty-year old Negro" dressed in a suit and tie is sitting alone on a subway car. Lula, a "thirty-year-old white woman" dressed "in bright, skimpy summer clothes and sandals" is a "tall, slender, beautiful woman with long red hair . . . eating an apple. . . ." She approaches him, provocatively, seductively, sadistically. Clay is aroused, wary, drawn in until she taunts him dancing, ". . . Come on, Clay. Let's do the nasty. Rub bellies. . . . Do the gritty grind, like your ol' rag-head mammy. . . ." Embarrassed he tries to make light of her antics, but she pushes on annoyed and agitated, ". . . Clay, you liver-lipped white man. . . . Clay, you got to break out. . . . Ol' Thomas Woolly-Head. . . . You black son of a bitch. . . ." At the height of her frenzied ranting he "slaps her as hard as he can, across the mouth . . . pushing her against the seat."

CLAY:

(*Pushing her against the seat.*)

I'm not telling you again, Tallulah Bankhead! Luxury. In your face and your fingers. You telling me what I ought to do.

(*Sudden scream frightening the whole coach.*)

Well, don't! Don't you tell me anything! If I'm a middle-class fake white man . . . let me be. And let me be in the way I want.

(*Through his teeth.*)

I'll rip your lousy breasts off! Let me be who I feel like being. Uncle Tom. Thomas. Whoever. It's none of your business. You don't know anything except what's there for you to see. An act. Lies. Device. Not the pure heart, the pumping black heart. You don't ever know that. And I sit here, in this buttoned-up suit, to keep myself from cutting all your throats. I mean wantonly. You great liberated whore! You fuck some black man, and right away you're an expert on black people. What a lotta shit that is. The only thing you know is that you come if he bangs you hard enough. And that's all. The belly rub? You wanted to do the belly rub? Shit, you don't even know how. You don't know how. That ol' dipty-dip shit you do, rolling your ass like an elephant. That's not my kind of belly rub. Belly rub is not Queens. Belly rub is dark places, with big hats and overcoats held up with one arm. Belly rub hates you. Old bald-headed four-eyed ofays popping their fingers . . . and don't know yet what they're doing. They say, "I love Bessie Smith." And don't even understand that Bessie Smith is saying, "Kiss my ass, kiss my black unruly ass." Before love, suffering, desire, anything you can explain, she's saying, and very plainly, "Kiss my black ass." And if you don't know that, it's you that's doing the kissing.

Charlie Parker? Charlie Parker. All the hip white boys scream for Bird. And Bird saying, "Up your ass, feebleminded ofay! Up your ass." And they sit there talking about the tortured genius of Charlie Parker. Bird would've played not a note of music if he just walked up to East Sixty-seventh Street and killed the first ten white people he saw. Not a note! And I'm the great would-be poet. Yes. That's right! Poet. Some kind of bastard literature . . . all it needs is a simple knife thrust. Just let me bleed you, you loud whore, and one poem vanished. A whole people of neurotics, struggling to keep from being sane. And the only thing that would cure the neurosis would be your murder. Simple as that. I mean if I murdered you, then other white people would begin to understand me. You understand? No. I guess not. If Bessie Smith had killed some white people she wouldn't have needed that music. She could have talked very straight and plain about the world. No metaphors. No grunts. No wiggles in the dark of her soul. Just straight two and two are four. Money. Power. Luxury. Like that. All of them. Crazy niggers turning their backs on sanity. When all it needs is that simple act. Murder. Just murder! Would make us all sane.

(*Suddenly weary.*)

Ahhh. Shit. But who needs it? I'd rather be a fool. Insane. Safe with my words, and no deaths, and clean, hard thoughts, urging me to new conquests. My people's madness. Hah! That's a laugh. My people. They don't need me to claim them. They got legs and arms of their own. Personal sanities. Mirrors. They don't need all those words. They don't need any defense. But listen, though, one more thing. And you tell this to your father, who's probably the kind of man who needs to know at once. So he can plan ahead. Tell him not to preach so much rationalism and cold logic to these niggers. Let them alone. Let them sing curses at you in code and see your filth as simple lack of style. Don't make the mistake, through some irresponsible surge of Christian charity, of talking too much about the advantages of Western rationalism, or the great intellectual legacy of the white man, or maybe they'll begin to listen. And then, maybe one day, you'll find they actually do understand exactly what you are talking about, all these fantasy people. All these blues people. And on that day, as sure as shit, when you really believe you can "accept" them into your fold, as half-white trusties late of the subject peoples. With no more blues, except the very old ones, and not a watermelon in sight, the great missionary heart will have triumphed, and all of those ex-coons will be stand-up Western men, with eyes for clean, hard, useful lives, sober, pious, and sane, and they'll murder you. They'll murder you, and have very rational explanations. Very much like your own. They'll cut your throats, and drag you out to the edge of your cities so the flesh can fall away from your bones, in sanitary isolation.

Education Is Our Right
Drew Hayden Taylor

Otter Lake, a fictional central Ontario reserve.

"*Education Is Our Right* was conceived, written and produced less than a year after Pierre Cadieux, then the Federal Minister of Indian and Northern Affairs (in Canada), announced a cap on post-secondary education for Native students." The play begins with Ebenezer Cadieux, the Minister of Indian Affairs, making the announcement of the cap on the Otter Lake reservation. After being confronted by a young woman who is trying to finish her college education, he is visited by the Spirit of Knowledge, who tells him he will be visited by three spirits. The Spirit of Education Past is "a tall, traditionally dressed (by Hollywood clichéd standards) Indian . . . arms folded, trying to look regal, like a cigar-store Indian . . . he talks like Tonto, monosyllabically. . .)." The Spirit takes him to see a television: "This is your television when boy. You spend many hours looking here. Saw many things, made you laugh, cry, scare you. . . . Including cowboys and Indians. . . ." Cadieux interjects with delight: "The Lone Ranger and Tonto, *Bonanza*, *Gunsmoke*! And all those movies. I remember them. . . . They all talked like you. . . ." The Spirit of Education Past then takes him to a ". . . small campfire. An old man and a young girl are sitting around it. It's a cold winter night and the two are huddled up in blankets or skins. The young girl, sitting enraptured by the old man, occasionally pokes the fire. . . . The Elder is in the midst of telling a legend to the young girl."

ELDER: And then one day this crazy old Nanabush was walking through the forest. He had trouble in his heart and mischief in his eyes. And in that forest he heard a noise, a small little noise, a peeping of a noise, and he stopped. He looked around but didn't see anything. But there was the mysterious peeping again, and it came from the sky. So Nanabush looked up and way up, I mean way up, was this bird's nest. Being naturally curious, Nanabush climbed to the top of that big tree, and do you know what he found? (*The little girl shakes her head.*) A nest full of little baby birds crying out for their mother. Now that Nanabush, with that mischief in his eyes, did something very silly. He thought to himself, "What do you do with a nest full of birds?" So he came to a conclusion. (*The little girl nods eagerly.*) He shit on them. Yep, that crazy old Nanabush took a shit on those poor defenseless birds and had a good laugh over it. In fact he laughed about it for a long time. Well, it wasn't over then. Later that summer Nanabush was out walking in that very same forest when he came to a stream. It wasn't a very big stream but it was wide enough to be annoying. So Nanabush decided to jump the stream. But to do that he had to clear a path and he spent all day preparing for that big jump. Near the end of that day he was ready. It took four tries before he knew he would make it, but as he was sailing over the stream he heard a voice call out his name. Nanabush looked up and boom, he lost his balance and went splash into the stream. He was a very wet and sorry-looking Nanabush. And those voices? Nanabush looked up and saw it was those very same birds that he had shit on not so long ago, but all were grown up and flying. They had the last laugh.

El Grito de las Minas
Anthony J. Garcia

Enrique Martinez is a New Mexican ranchero now forced to be a miner, in 1904. He is separated from the wife and family he loves. Sara has taught him to read, and his letter is a mixture of loneliness, love, and an awkward but passionate phrasing that is at times eloquent. He is a humble man who at times is overcome by the immensity of the ideas that he is expressing. Athough the monologue is primarily in English, it should be understood that Enrique is writing in Spanish.

ENRIQUE: My most precious Sara, tonight I looked into the naked blackness of the sky and saw your face. Suddenly the stars rose up to reflect your eyes, causing shadow to shape the curve of your cheekbones, a present at birth from your Apache grandmother.

I am ever grateful to you for the life that you have given me. Because of you, I can write these words on the pages that will carry my love to you. Because of you, I can read the words that you send me. Yes, I miss making love to you. I miss the, "ends of the afternoon," as you call them. I miss that my son is no longer innocent and that now he works alongside me, here in the darkness beneath the earth.

It is difficult for a man who has worked in sunlight all his life to face day upon day, entering the mines in darkness and leaving them well after the sun has left the sky. The money I send you is from the script that I have been able to sell. The company does not pay us in money, so what I send you is what I am able to get, and that sadly is often only fifty cents on the dollar. The three of us, Elias, Pepe, and myself, share a room with fourteen other miners, so we have all become pretty close. Although the distance and separation have been painful, I thank you for not insisting on traveling with me. I look forward to seeing you at Christmas. The three of us will leave the mines. If only for that short time we will be a family together.

Sara, sometimes I think that should death trap me, and my heart be forced to spend eternity inside this mountain, you must not mourn. You once told me that when you were a young girl your mother took you to the Catholic Nuns, to provided you with the skills to read and write. You were allowed to know the great books. With your mother's blessing you were being prepared to be an educated bride of Christ. Instead, I am blessed that you became the bride of a *ranchero*.

Siempre en tu vida,

Tu esposo Enrique

Fierce Love: Stories from Black Gay Life
**Pomo Afro Homos
(Postmodern African-American Homosexuals)
Brian Freeman, Djola Branner, and Eric Gupton**

"Silently Into the Night"

The Pomo Afro Homos created this ensemble piece to tell the stories of black gay men who are "numerous and varied, flamboyant and dull, pious, perverse . . . the who's who and the who's not . . . cruel and loving, tight-assed and loose . . . unlike and similar to all the age old myths . . . an endangered species. . . . But our stories must be told . . . our lives forever real must be cherished and our love forever rising must be has got to be no doubt about it as strong as our ancestors' and twice as fierce."

DJOLA (*AS HE ENTERS HE SINGS "YOU ARE MY FRIEND" LIKE PATTI LABELLE*): He was my boon-coon buddy, my main man, my best girlfriend. I mean we ate, drank, sang, danced, prayed, cried, and screamed together. We had to quit hanging so tight 'cause everyone thought we were lovers and neither of us could get any play. But I loved me some Aman.

I worked only two blocks from the hospital, so I spent my lunch hours with Aman during those last three weeks. And I remember this particular morning I woke up and decided I wouldn't wait until lunch to see him. I would go in before I went to the office. He was in ICU by then. The respirator was going. He was in a coma. Had been for a couple of days. Even in the stillness, there was such pain in the room. And I just stood there, watching his chest rise and fall, and pretty soon I was breathing in the same time, our last dance you might say, 'cause everything else in the room was suspended. I felt him rise out of his skin and drape one of those lanky arms around me. Funny, I thought, here he was consoling me. We were communicating somehow, and I looked at his body, heaving, and said, "Well, girl, this is another fine mess you've gotten yourself into." He laughed, withdrew his arm, and slunk back into his skin.

I looked up from the computer just before lunch and thought about Aman. Felt him. When I stopped by the hospital after work, the nurse told me he had passed away around noon.

My friend Bolla a.k.a. Miss Process, the Margaret Meade of psychic healing, picked up Aman's mother at the airport. She knew she was trouble the minute she stepped off the plane with that gray hair piled high as the control tower and those patent leather pumps, and bag to match. Aman hadn't seen his mama in eleven years but she quickly set about the task of laying him to rest. She let Bolla pick the outfit to lay him out in. She chose that nice bright Guatemalan shirt, the one I gave him, some turquoise drawstring pants, and a sharp African crown for his head.

Now if the hippies who burnt sage and dangled crystals all over the man while he was in the hospital thought Mama was spooky— they swore that the oldest brother, who Aman hadn't seen in *thirteen* years, was a monster. A fundamentalist Lutheran preacher, who felt it was his duty, especially since mother had summoned him, to preside over the funeral. Six foot one and every inch a Christian as Aman was queer. If you knew Aman you know that was some serious faith. The brother made arrangements to have the funeral at a mortuary in Bayview Hunter's Point.

It was a *long* drive out to Bayview. Me and Lance, my hippie, my lover, drove behind the family limo. The first mile was quiet. Then we came to a stoplight at 16th & Mission and this huge Negro in a white suit and red shirt, hair greasy enough to stir-fry broccoli in, steps from the curb. I don't know this man from Adam but he opens the door and jumps into the back seat. Explains that he has been invited to speak at the funeral by Aman's brother, who is riding in the limo up ahead. I look at Lance, he looks at me, and as the stoplight changes from red to green the Negro prays silently to himself. The car reeks of Aqua Velva.

(ERIC *and* BRIAN *enter singing "Precious Lord."*)

DJOLA: (*over song*) Once in the mortuary, I wonder if I can get through the service. Get through the mother, who has asked me to take pictures with her Kodak Instamatic, and especially through the brother, who is on a mission of his own. (*Becoming the brother.*) "There were so many questions in my heart as I began this journey to San Francisco. Why had Aman and I grown estranged? Why had over a decade passed since we laid eyes upon each other? Why had we—like Cain and Abel—been unable to confer our love as flesh, as family upon one another? Yes, so many questions in my heart. And in my search for answers the Lord in his wisdom led me to my hometown church's sister congregation over in Oakland. In that temple of worship, a man was referred to me by his most generous pastor, a man who might provide some hard-sought answers. In his mercy, that gentleman is with us today and has consented to speak." Now, ninety percent of the congregation is lesbian and gay. People are sighing. Seriously sighing as Mazola head, the man in the white suit, strides to the altar. (*Becoming the man.*) "I didn't know Aman, so I can't comment on his life, but my life, too, was filled with desire.

Every minute of every waking day was a living hell because all I thought about was having my way with men. And before God I can't lie, I *had* my way with *many* men. I could not get through the day without visiting the Pendulum, or the Blue & Gold—that's closed now, or the dirty bookstores, the Eagle Creek—that reopened, the Steamworks, or the toilets at the library, or the northside of Lake Merritt. But I *have* found Jesus, and there is comfort in his hand." The brother shouts, "Repent!" Mama shouts, "Amen!" And I can't take it anymore! I am gone, down the aisle, out the front door, and into the street.

(ERIC *and* BRIAN *exit.*)

I want a cigarette, it's been three months but I would really like a cigarette. Lance follows me into the street. Why does he look so fucking calm? But before I can say anything fifteen, twenty, thirty people pour into the street, some crying, others pulling their hair, others screaming. We are a collective mess. I decide after *two* margaritas that a cigarette definitely will not resolve the hurt. Or the anger. I call my sister in L.A. and threaten to haunt the bitch for the rest of her natural life if she ever pulls a stunt like that. We organize another memorial service—minus the blood relatives. I sing, Miss Process lights candles, and we bid a fond farewell to Aman's spirit at the ocean. And I wonder, why do so many of our brothers bundle up their pain and go off silently into the night?

(*He sings as he exits. Blackout.*)

Fires in the Mirror
Anna Deavere Smith

"101 Dalmations" George C. Wolfe

Anna Deavere Smith's one-woman play *Fires in the Mirror* is one of a series of works from her *On the Road* project, which utilizes interview theater techniques to probe conflicts or themes within a specific community. *Fires in the Mirror* examines the controversy surrounding the 1991 Crown Heights riots in Brooklyn, New York, between blacks and Hasidic Jews. In the first section of the play, entitled "Identity," she prefaces the riots with perspectives of a number of people, famous and unknown, black and white, Jewish and gentile, who engage the issue of racial and cultural identity.

The setting for this interview with director/playwright George C. Wolfe was "The Mondrian Hotel in Los Angeles. Morning. Sunny. A very nice room. George is wearing denim jeans, a light blue denim shirt and white leather tennis shoes. His hair is in a ponytail. He wears tortoise/wire spectacles. He is drinking tea with milk. The tea is served on a tray, the cups and teapot are delicate porcelain. George is sitting on a sofa, with his feet up on the coffee table."

I mean I grew up on a black—
a one-block street—

that was black.
My grandmother lived on that street
my cousins lived around the corner.
I went to this
Black—Black—
private Black grade school
where
I was extraordinary.
Everybody there was extraordinary.
You were told you were extraordinary.
It was very clear
that I could not go to see *101 Dalmations* at the Capital
     Theatre
because it was segregated.
And at the same time
I was treated like I was the most extraordinary creature
     that had
been born.
So I'm on my street in my house,
at my school—
and I was very spoiled too—
so I was treated like I was this special special creature.
And then I would go beyond a certain point
I was treated like I was insignificant.
Nobody was
hosing me down or calling me nigger.
It was just that I was insignificant.
(*Slight pause*)
You know what I mean so it was very clear of
(*Teacup on saucer strike twice on "very clear"*)
where my extraordinariness lived.

You know what I mean.
That I was extraordinary as long as I was Black.
But I am—not—going—to place myself
(*Pause*)
in relationship to your whiteness.
I will talk about your whiteness if we want to talk about that.
But I,
but what,
that which,
what I—
what am I saying?
My blackness does not resis—ex—re—
exist in relationship to your whiteness.
(*Pause*)
You know
(*Not really a question, more like a hum*)
(*Slight pause*)
it does not exist in relationship to—
it *exists*
it exists.
I come—
you know what I mean—
like I said, I, I, I,
I come from—
it's a very com*plex*,
con*fused*,
neu-rotic,
at times destructive
reality, but it is completely
and totally a reality
contained and, and,

and full unto itself.
It's complex.
It's demonic.
It's ridiculous.
It's absurd.
It's evolved.
It's all the stuff.
That's the way I grew up.
(*Slight pause*)
So that *therefore*—
and then you're White—
(*Quick beat*)
And then there's a point when,
and then these two things come into contact.

The First Breeze of Summer
Leslie Lee

Act 1. A small city in the Northeast on a Thursday afternoon in June.

As Gremmar, a black woman in her seventies, approaches death in the middle of a summer that has not yet "had a decent breeze," she remembers the people who played important roles in her life. A string of pearls she has transports her back to when she was seventeen. The pearls were a gift from her beau, Sam Green, a black man in his mid- to late twenties who worked as a porter at the train station in town. After giving her the necklace, he lets on that he was fired from his job two days before and that now he has to leave or "stay here and . . . starve." In this monologue, he tells why he was fired and the misery that he feels as a result of losing his job.

SAM: He couldn't make it, baby. You have to eat. What are you going to eat—promises? Damn right we get sick. But who the hell can pay for it? He couldn't make it. The man had to eat! A hell of a lot of sick people, but no cash, babe! Colored people weren't ready for colored doctors, or maybe colored doctors weren't ready for colored people. I forget the way he put it, but something like that. . . . He said he didn't mind helping folks, but he didn't realize how much it was necessary for him not to be hungry—to not be worrying about next month all the time . . . (*Pauses.*) Wanted it simple, he said . . . just plain simple, you know, babe. . . . Didn't want to have to think . . . or feel . . . or even care . . . the hell with it. . . . Gave it up . . . He's a porter, so help me God, a porter, down at the station. (*Pause.*) He was . . . you know . . . doing his job. . . . He's pushing this cracker's bags . . . Cracker's got enough bags for everybody in this whole town piled up on top of Pop's cart. He's pushing the damn thing, and it's heavy, but he's pushing, smiling and whistling, happy-like. . . . And I don't know, for some reason one of the bags comes tumbling down and falls on the floor. The thing is, it splits—A couple of things break. The cracker claims they're from—I don't know whether he's lying or not—from Paris or Europe, one of them damn places. And all of a sudden he's getting red in the face. He's yelling and making a big stew, calling Doc names! Calling him boy this and nigger that, and Pop—Pop is just . . . just standing there—like he's supposed to take it, smiling and apologizing. (*Pause.*) He's got his mind—Pop—on what he is now, not what he was. He ain't no goddamn porter, but he don't want nobody to change it. He's got it all figured out! So that stupid, dumb, doctor-porter is taking all the cracker's crap! Taking it, talking to himself, reciting that stuff from his medical books! . . . Well, I couldn't take it! So I hightail it over to where they standing, and—and before I could catch myself, I'm telling this cracker off! I got my hand, my fist, my nose into his, and I'm screaming at him— yelling at him—calling him the names he's calling Pop. And that stupid Pop—Doc—is pulling at me—yanking at me, because he knows, because he's made it all so simple! And he's struggling with me! And I'm yelling at the cracker: "This man's a doctor, goddammit! You oughta be carrying his bags, you sonofabitch! Don't you talk to Dr. Savage that way! And Pop is crying almost, because I promised I wouldn't say nothing to nobody! That's what's getting him! He's begging me and half crying for me to shut up! And then all of a sudden he pulls out that damn piece of paper and tears it into shreds—just rips it up! (*Pauses.*) Well . . . to make a long story short . . . that's it. I mean, that's it . . . I wasn't worth a good minute after that. . . . Right on the spot . . . on the damn spot! (*Pauses*) I turn around . . . on my way out . . . and there's . . . *Pop* . . . doing penance for me . . . cleaning up that bastard's shit . . . smiling, apologizing . . . kissing ass! . . . If he's mad, he's mad at me and not at the cracker—for messing up his goddamn, stupid world. . . . (*Laughing suddenly and sitting in the chair stage center.*) Baby, I'm so miserable, it's funny . . . miserable . . .

Fish Head Soup
Philip Kan Gotanda

Act 3. Second scene. At the river's edge, a town in the San Joaquin Valley, California, 1989.

Mat Iwasaki is a Japanese American in his late twenties to early thirties. At the play's beginning we see the Iwasaki family at Mat's funeral, an event which begins the downward physical and mental spiral of his father, Togo "Papa" Iwasaki. Mat appears in the next scene, returning home several years after what we learn was a faked drowning and disappearance in the river where his father used to fish. An actor, desperate to make a film with an Asian American focus, Mat has returned home to borrow money to finance the project. He discovers a family shattered by the after-math of his "death": his father is an incoherent invalid, his brother Victor is a Vietnam veteran suffering from post-traumatic shock, and his mother is having an affair. Unable to convince his mother to help him and unable to get through to his mentally ill father, he eventually loses the other backers of the film. With his project dead, he wheels his invalid father to the water's edge.

MAT: Remember that time downtown? Are you listening to me? Are you listening? Remember that time downtown when that big guy came up to you? "Hey, you a China-man?" You mumbled something and pushed Victor and me into the back seat of the car. You had this funny look on your face,—: all tight. "No, no, excuse me." Victor and I had our noses pressed against the window waiting for you to yell at this ugly man. To put this ugly mean man in his place. "What, you one of those people from Ja-pan? You a Jap?" He was laughing and having a good time, a crowd had gathered. You finally got in the car but the man was lying on the hood now. I kept thinking, "Why isn't Papa yelling like he does at home or when Mr. Nakamura fixes the car wrong?" But you just sat there, stiff, staring ahead.

Are you listening to me?

All the way home, no one said anything. And I remember my face feeling all hot. Feeling ashamed. Victor and I never talked about it. And I began to hate you. Hate you because you were my daddy and every time I looked at you I saw you being humiliated, shuffling like a houseboy in front of that man. And you made me feel that same feeling.

So, I hung out with whites. Yes, I made fun of other "oriental" kids, cracked jokes about them—hell, I wasn't one of them. I mean, why would I want to be like one of those quiet shuffling cowards? Why would I want to be like my papa? Papa who sits here while Mama goes off and. . .

And so one night I left. Nah, one night I killed myself. Yes, I just killed myself off.

(*Pause.*)

But Papa? I'm back. And you gotta help me this time. This time, you gotta help me, you can't leave me in the back seat. Papa? You owe (*grabbing* PAPA *by shirt and shaking him*) me. *You owe me!* YOU OWE ME!

for black boys who have considered homicide when the streets were too much
Keith Antar Mason

Keith Antar Mason's choreopoem, inspired by ntozake shange's *for colored girls who have considered suicide when the rainbow was enuf* brings voices of black men, their desires, rage, pain, and love to a ritualized space in the theater. Identifying the characters as numbers, "in basic training . . . on the corner . . . at howard university . . . in a tomb . . . in hot water, mississippi . . . takin' numbers any number niggers are . . . jus'numbers any age. . . ." Brother #3, "angry, furious," indicts a society which has labeled him as a menace to be feared.

BROTHER #3:

i must be mistaken
some monster
i know
i can tell by the way you look
at me
you tighten up
and never smile
like aggression can only
be symbolized

69

by me
like the male gender
and colored black means
death carrier
potent poison
lethal
like the only mind i
have is between
my legs
and all it does is piss
the sewage out
the raw unadulterated
mean-ness
and i know
some how i know
i want to live
a long time but
i am gonna die
some obscene
joke
cuz' you clutch
yourself around me
hold back
all the good things
even precious smiles
from me
some how i know
i wuz' born to die
to die too soon
and i don't understand

and that's the confusion you see
that's the fear
you feel
i am no more than
the stacked up
cemented
aggression
black tornado
come back from
oz no hell
born to die
and i mus' be
a zombie
walkin' the streets
the livin' dead
and my brain
my dick
the curse
    of the male gender
colored black
colored black
with nappy hair

and you only feel
afraid
but i know
how fear kills
i know
i live it
standin'
on the corner

holdin' the wall
like a firin' squad
and some how i know
i wuz' born to die
a zombie
live or dead
the male gender
cursed
colored black
and too damn
aggressive
jus' by being born

49
Hanay Geiogamah

Scene 10. A ceremonial ground circa 1885 and the same ceremonial ground in the present.

Night Walker is "the ceremonial leader of the tribe," of any age. The play takes play at a 49 celebration, which usually begins "about midnight or just after, when the more formal activities of the powwow or Indian fair or tribal celebration are over. . . . Forty-nines always take place at night; really good ones go on until sunrise and after. More young people are involved than older ones, and thus the scene is charged with the energy of hundreds of youths. . . . While taking part in a 49, young Indians are in an extremely heightened state of awareness of their "Indianness". . . the environment is intertribal, and the dangers of "police harassment, jailing, automobile accidents, and injuries from fighting" are present.

Throughout the play, the shaman figure of Night Walker "creates the tie between the young people's past and their present and future. He can move supernaturally between both eras and speak directly to both generations. Night Walker is probably a little disappointed that nothing more solid and serious than 49 has emerged for the young Indians, but he is always optimistic, never without hope." At the point of Night Walker's story, a car accident has just occurred and a girl lies on the stage floor.

NIGHT WALKER: (*to the young people grouped around him*) This arbor cannot be killed. It is strong and powerful. It has lived for a very long time. It can be burned and torn apart, but its life cannot be taken from it. It draws its life from the hearts and souls of the tribe, our people.

There was a time in the journey of our people, when the power of the arbor had lost much of its strength.

My grandmother told me the story of this time in our people's journey. An old woman from another place came into the village. She played with the children, who thought she was silly and harmless. She was given a tipi to stay in while she visited.

One night, she invited all of the children of the tribe to her tipi to tell them stories of the land from where she had come.

The children begged her to tell them more; her stories were the kind that young people like to hear.

She told them that if they wanted to go to her country she would take them. They had to promise her that they would do everything that she told them to do. They all agreed.

The smoke from her fire became thick. The old woman told the children to put their hands into the smoke, and the smoke would carry them up through the flap of the tipi and out over the night sky to her land. They agreed to forget all of the ways of our people while they were on the journey.

The children were eager to go to her country. They did as the old lady told them to do, and one by one their figures and voices disappeared from the circle around the fire.

One of the mothers of the tribe went to the tipi to bring her children back to her camp. She cried out when she saw the tipi was empty. The fire was still burning.

The tribespeople became angry. The chiefs had young warriors guard the tipi. A prayer meeting was held. The ceremonial leader sought a vision.

All the tribe crowded around our arbor to hear him tell of what he had seen.

"The children are still in the tipi," the good man told the tribespeople. "The old lady visitor played a trick on them. She promised to take them to her country. But she is the only one who could leave the tipi. The children are safe, they are warm, they are singing and dancing, playing games and telling stories. None of them is quarelling with the others."

"But the tipi is empty, our children are dead, they have been stolen!" the tribespeople cried out. The mothers began to wail.

"They are in the tipi," the old man repeated.

The people did not believe him. They said his vision was wrong. The chiefs pulled in the horses and formed the braves into groups to search for the lost children. The men rode off, leaving only the old people and the women. The wise man stayed under the arbor, praying.

He prayed for many seasons.

The women would not look at him. They wanted to burn the tipi, but he said they would have to kill him if they did. They were afraid to harm the holy man, and he still prayed.

Then the hunting parties began to return to the camp. The men had ridden far in all directions. Their grief was strong for their lost children. They had changed as men.

None of the tribespeople would come to the arbor.

The wise man saw that the fire, which had not stopped burning, had started to go out.

He carried firewood to the tipi and waited outside until the fire had nearly died out. Some of the tribespeople gathered around to watch. The holy man went into the tipi with the firewood and started the fire again. When the flames began to jump from the burning wood, the wise man started to sing. The smoke began rising up

75

through the flap. Many tribespeople were outside the tipi now, watching and talking among themselves.

Suddenly, many voices could be heard singing, the voices of the children. The singing got louder. From outside the tipi the tribespeople could see in now. They saw the figures of their children take shape through the light. The wise man led the singing children out of the tipi and into the arms of their mothers and fathers. The people cried out in happiness.

The wise man led all the people to the arbor. One of the older boys stood to talk before all of the tribe. "We have been inside the tipi," he said. "We could see all of you, but you could not see us. We could not come out until you believed that we were inside. We sang, danced, used the colors." He showed them a pretty breastplate that he had made. "We have changed," he told the tribe. "We are better men and women now."

Night Walker strikes the drum a single hit, then a second one, and the injured girl rises from the stage floor and joins the group.

The tribespeople painted the tipi with beautiful colors and designs. They placed many gifts under the arbor. The arbor once again was covered with the beautiful light of its love for the people.

The Gate of Heaven
Lane Nishikawa and Victor Talmadge

Act 2. Scene 4. Leon's office. 1983.

Kiyoshi "Sam" Yamamoto is a Japanese American Nisei (second genera-
tion) from Hawai'i who, during the course of the play, ages from twenty to
seventy, his Hawai'ian pidgin accent gradually fading. The play begins on
April 29, 1945, the day the Dachau concentration camp was liberated. As
one of the Japanese American soldiers who participated in the liberation
of the Dachau survivors, we first see Sam with Leon, an emaciated Jewish
internee, near death. Leon, seeing an Asian face, is confused and deliri-
ous, at first believing that Japanese troops have arrived.

Ten years later, we find Leon, now a medical Army officer, in the Presidio
U.S. Army base in San Francisco. He has been searching for and has finally
found Sam, his liberator. Unbeknownst to Leon, Sam received an unde-
served military discharge for conduct unbecoming a noncommissioned
officer. Their second meeting in 1955 begins a lifelong friendship that
tests the boundaries of cultural difference. In this scene, nearly forty years
after their dramatic first meeting, Sam finally reveals why he was dis-
charged. His story is told to Leon and in a flashback to at the U.S. Senate
hearings on Japanese American Redress and Reparations.

SAM: When I came home from Europe, I stopped off in New York City. It was my first time in the Big Apple. We had just left this kind of a "thank you" event given by the Japanese community. I had on my dress uniform with my medals on my chest. I was so proud because none of the old men and women had ever seen a Silver Star before. It was hanging right next to my Purple Hearts. (*Pause.*) I guess I was kind of a celebrity. (*Sam crosses downstage. Lights crossfade to a spot on Sam, now at the Redress Hearings in Washington, D. C.*) My neck was sore from looking up at the skyscrapers. My buddies from the 422 and I got off the subway at midtown around 47th Street and Broadway, and walked into the best restaurant we could find. We hadn't had an American meal for nearly two years. We asked for a booth and were seated. I could just taste the big T-bone steak I was about to order. The waiter came over to our table with the restaurant manager. They told us we had to leave. They didn't serve Japs at their establishment. I couldn't believe what I was hearing. I couldn't even breathe. I looked around the restaurant at the other customers and you know what. . .they were laughing at us. My buddies looked at me wondering what to do. I had the highest rank at the table. A couple of people started throwing food from their plates yelling, "Remember Pearl Harbor!" I stood up and nodded to my men and we marched toward the door. Everyone we passed threw their drinks at us. Then a bunch of guys charged at us screaming, "Japs go home!" (*Clears his throat.*) The Police Department turned us over to the MPs. They charged us with being drunk and disorderly and instigating a public disturbance. We had put two guys in the hospital. They held us responsible for the property damage. It was the word of everyone in that restaurant against the six of us. The Army said we were a disgrace to the uniform. I told them since I was the ranking soldier I would take full responsibility. My commanding officer called me into his office. He was a man I knew and trusted. He told me the court wanted to set an example and was considering taking away my rank; they were talking full court martial proceedings; they were talking dishonorable discharge; but . . . if I resigned, all of the charges would be dropped. My record would be kept intact. (*Pause.*) The Army gave us a chance to prove ourselves when America was pointing the finger at our patriotism. The Army allowed us to be men. The Army was going to be my life. (*Recites from memory.*) "By direction of the President of the United States, for Gallantry, in connection with military operations against a hostile force, Sergeant Kiyoshi Yamamoto distinguished himself by heroic action." What they couldn't take were my medals. We weren't drunk. We just wanted a meal. We were so glad finally to be home. (Senators, I love this country. I'm an American. You have to pass this reparations bill. You can't let this happen again. Thank you.)

(*Lights fade to black.*)

I Am a Man
OyamO

Act 1. Retail Clerks, Union Hall. Memphis, Tennessee. Early February 1968.
Sunday Evening.

Ollie Jones is an African American man, age forty, who is heading the
effort to organize sanitation workers in the city of Memphis following the
tragic death of two black sanitation workers. He "speaks with vocal, ges-
tural and emotional ebullience." He is "beefy, but average height, very
friendly, but also bullheaded about some things. Somewhat vulnerable, a
bit fearful and not well educated, [he] quit Memphis Public School in the
8th grade." A tireless leader who neglects his family for his cause, he is
"naturally intelligent—[possessing] common street sense, a cajoling wit,
a generous nature, and a lot of heart." In this early scene, Jones appears
before hundreds of outraged and grieving men at a union meeting.
Recounting in vivid detail how their brother workers died, he appeals to
the men to go on strike.

JONES: Day come ta work that day, but it was rainin' bad. Thunda and
lightnin' storm, and da rain, it look like da whole Mississippi pourin'
down on Memphis. Day don't let ya wuck in the rain. Got ta wait 'till
the rain finish and maybe you get a few hours wuck. The men gon'
wait fah da rain ta stop. So da garage foe'men, he cain't have no cullud peepas sittin' in the garage where da white folks sit. So the two

cullud wuckers went to sit in da garbage truck in the yard. Alright. Da truck cab locked up. Can't git in dere. Day go to the foe'men. Foe'man tell 'em day cain't sit in the garage wit da white crew chiefs. Day just hafta wait in the rain. Foe'men, say: "Ya'll sit in the back of da truck. It's dry. Plenty room back dere. Ain't picked up no garbage yet." Alright. So da two men go ta sit in the back of the truck in the bailer where day loads the garbage. Day sit-tin' back dere when lightnin' strike the truck and make the bailer machinery start up by itsef. Da men strugglin' ta get out foe day gits crushed; day scream-ing fa help, but da thunda cover day screams. Cain't nobody hear dem. The machinery done crush da men ta deaf' foe anybody knowed what happen. Machinery was broke in the fust place and the foe'man knowed it. Foe'men knowed dat bailer lahble ta start anytime. But he ain't care; he ain't care about dese two cullud mens. He cain't hear day screams while day dying. So our two union brothas is gone, and da family grievin' 'cause day don't know what da future holin' fa dem. It's winta in Memphis, and fah dese two fam-ilies it's gon' be winta for a long time. We got to hep dem like as if day was our own family.

(*Reaches into pocket and pulls out money and ceremoniously counts it into his hat, passes the hat to* SOMEONE *who carries it off-stage.*)

I hole onta half my paycheck from the union. I hole onta half my check, 'cause I knowed the family gon' need our hep in dis time of day grief and mournin'. Let's all search our hearts and pocketbooks an' fine even just a few pennies. Let's do it now and spare these fam-ilies mo' grief. While we doin' dat, let's talk about action.

I Hate
Bernardo Solano

I Hate is a self-contained monologue.

Andres is a Colombian American, and as the stories he tells are memories, he can be anywhere from his early twenties to late forties. He is address- ing a stranger who has brought up the true incident of a Colombian soc- cer player who was killed for accidentally scoring a goal against his own team. As Andres tries to make sense of it all, he is reminded of several childhood memories.

ANDRES: And in that dark Colombian parking lot . . . they shot him. Thanks for scoring the goal for the U.S. and here's a bullet for your trouble. Goal—boom. Goal—boom. Boom, bang, bang . . . die. Jesus Christ, how many bullets is it going to take before we stop doing this? But this time we've done it in front of the whole world. A guy from Colombia whose only crime was to play a sport for his country. And here we are, those of us Colombians who've been raised here in the U.S., those of us who have spent most of our lives enduring wave after wave of stupid jokes, whether they be about marijuana in the '70s, cocaine in the '80s, or a serape-clad musta- chioed-man and his donkey peddling coffee throughout. How can I possibly celebrate being from a country that the world now knows mostly for an especially cruel brand of violence? What's there to be proud of? All I feel right now is a sadness that weighs me down, makes me sink into the mud.

(*Pause*)

Let me tell you about what happened to me in ninth grade. We had just moved to the suburbs and it was my first year in high school. There were maybe a dozen ethnic students in the whole school. It's a Saturday and I'm at a football game. I don't know anybody yet so I find it very easy to wander off on my own. I go inside the school to get a drink of water and I'm standing at the water fountain. A much larger anglo kid walks right up to me and asks me what I would do if he hit me in the face. (*Sighs*) I consider running for a moment, but for some reason that doesn't seem like a good idea. I guess I could kick him in the nuts and *then* run, but that doesn't seem so smart either. A big part of me wants to ask him who the hell he thinks I am, I mean, what did I do to deserve the random act of violence I see fast approaching. But I don't ask. Another option comes to mind: Scream. Scream your head off hoping someone will come to the rescue, and then run. I don't know why I keep coming back to the running thing. An eternity has passed. Five seconds have come and gone. What would I do if he hit me in the face? Nothing. And that's what I say to him: "Nothing. . . ." For a brief moment he's taken aback by my response. Am I being a chicken shit? Or am I challenging him? I can tell he's not sure which. Which makes two of us. Whatever the case, he decides he's not going to back down, that he can't back down. With no further delay he winds up and delivers a freckled fist right between my eyes. My head snaps back and my vision blurs. And I stand there. Motionless. I neither hit back, nor do I run. Nor do I cry. Again he's surprised. And to cover his surprise he laughs a quick "you are fucking crazy" kind of laugh and saunters off. And I'm still standing there.

A Jamaican Airman Foresees His Death
Fred D'Aguiar

Act 1. Scene 3. Jamaica. An enlistment interview. World War II.

Alvin, a young Jamaican, is a rear gunner in the Royal Air Force stationed in Scotland. He is being called a "killer" and is being investigated for having shot down an aircraft from his own squadron. The only one of his group of Jamaican fellow enlistees to be allowed to fly (the others were relegated to jobs as cooks, janitors, etc.), he is defended by his countrymen: "I bet the white boys don't get harassed when they make a mistake. . . . They shot at you. What were you supposed to do, wait and check if they got a pilot's license before you fire back?" In this flashback to his enlistment interview, Alvin expands on his boyhood fascination and longing for flight.

Alvin: When I was a boy, my uncle made me a kite, nearly as tall as me. But when I raised it I was too small to control it. A grown-up had to hold my arms to stop it dragging me away. One day I decided to fly the kite on my own. I was sure if I got the right grip and a sure foothold I could steer it—have fingertip control, like I did with smaller kites. I raised it all right. There was a good breeze and the principle is the same whatever the kite-size. I thought I was on top of it—on top of it and on top of the world. I began to jump up and down. I even called out for everyone to come and see me, Alvin, behind that kite they all thought I'd have to give away. Just then a strong breeze hit the kite. Something pulled me so hard I had to look up. All I saw way up in the sky was this tadpole waving. I thought that small thing can't tug with so much force, it must be the hand of God. I thought, if I could hold on long enough, I'd be hauled up to heaven. And heaven to me was all the things I ever wanted but could never have: shoes, long trousers, black pudding, pepper-pot and souse every day, a new slate for school. Things I dreamed about. Things I knew I would have when I got to heaven. We used to make long lists. We talked to God, but he never replied. When he did answer some people in church we could never understand what they were saying. I tried running along with the pull, but my legs weren't fast enough. I heard the shouts of let go, let go, but I couldn't let go of heaven. I held on for dear life. When I came round they told me I was dragged into a fence. It took me a long time to believe what the preacher preaching on Sundays and even longer to get round to praying. But I never doubted for a moment that I had to fly. Not to God. But because in my head that kite's still up there, waiting for me to pilot it to the ground.

Joe Turner's Come and Gone
August Wilson

Act 2. Scene 2. The parlor of a boardinghouse in Pittsburgh. August, 1911.

The play is set in a time when "newly freed African slaves wander into the city . . . isolated, cut off from memory . . . they arrive carrying Bibles and guitars, their pockets lined with dust and fresh hope. . . ." Bynum Walker, is "a short, round man in his early sixties. A conjure man, or rootworker, he gives the impression of always being in control of everything. Nothing ever bothers him. He seems to be lost in a world of his own making and to swallow any adversity or interference with his grand design." He lives at the boardinghouse of Seth Holly, "born of free parents, a skilled craftsman."

In this scene, Bynum confronts Herald Loomis, a newcomer to the boardinghouse, a mysterious and volatile figure, who is "at times possessed. A man driven not by the hellhounds that seemingly bay at his heels, but by his search for a world that speaks to something about himself. He is unable to harmonize the forces that swirl around him, and seeks to recreate that world into one that contains his image. . . ."

Bynum: I can tell from looking at you. My daddy taught me how to do that. Say when you look at a fellow, if you taught yourself to look for it, you can see his song written on him. Tell you what kind of man he is in the world. Now, I can look at you, Mr. Loomis, and see you a man who done forgot his song. Forgot how to sing it. A fellow forget that and he forget who he is. Forget how he's supposed to mark down life. Now, I used to travel all up and down this road and that . . . looking here and there. Searching. Just like you, Mr. Loomis. I didn't know what I was searching for. The only thing I knew was something was keeping me dissatisfied. Something wasn't making my heart smooth and easy. Then one day my daddy gave me a song. That song had a weight to it that was hard to handle. That song was hard to carry. I fought against it. Didn't want to accept that song. I tried to find my daddy to give him back the song. But I found out it wasn't his song. It was my song. It had come from way deep inside me. I looked long back in memory and gathered up pieces and snatches of things to make that song. I was making it up out of myself. And that song helped me on the road. Made it smooth to where my footsteps didn't bite back at me. All the time that song getting bigger and bigger. That song growing with each step of the road. It got so I used all of myself up in the making of that song. Then I was the song in search of itself. That song rattling in my throat and I'm looking for it. See, Mr. Loomis, when a man forgets his song he goes off in search of it . . . till he find out he's got it with him all the time. That's why I can tell you one of Joe Turner's niggers. 'Cause you forgot how to sing your song.

A Language of Their Own
Chay Yew

"Randy in the Afternoons"

Ming is a "twentysomething Asian Male, speaks American English." His former lover Oscar is a "thirtysomething Asian male, speaks English with a slight unobtrusive accent." Oscar has AIDS; the play begins with the two men explaining why Oscar has asked Ming to move out, after four years of living together and examining what their subsequent interaction has been. "Oscar and Ming often speak to the audience, as if they were lawyers defending different points of view on the same case." Their dialogue reveals differences in character and culture—"Ming: We were polite even when we broke up. We've always been so fucking polite to each other. Please. Thank you. You're welcome. After you. . . . I don't know when I stopped learning how to speak Chinese. Everyone at school spoke English beautifully and my English was always—well, unrefined, pidgin, tainted. The stuff Rex Harrison sang of in *My Fair Lady* . . . I think *My Fair Lady* was pivotal in my life. It taught me how to speak proper English, appreciate good clothes, and made me realize I was gay. . . . " Ming loves Oscar, but the introduction of Oscar's illness in their lives is something he cannot cope with.

Since breaking up with Oscar, Ming has become involved with Robert, a white male, and has moved from Boston to Venice, California. Although happy with Robert, he is restless and still haunted by his relationship with Oscar, and he tells Robert that they should see other people, "Nothing's going to change. Nothing . . . it's not you. It's me. . . ." Ming searches for anonymity in bathhouses and with strangers like Randy, while being unable to avoid the vivid associations of his two lovers.

MING: I receive Randy's message on my voice mail
I hear him say, "Same place at one"
I drive, in the blistering heat, as if given a
    command
I'm half-shaking with anticipation, half-annoyed at
    his barking message
I arrive, in a bathhouse, in Hollywood
I get myself a locker
I wrap myself with a white towel smelling
    faintly of bleach
I walk barefoot to our usual room, at the end of
    the floor
I see him there, lying on a narrow bed, with a
    half-open door
I see him, naked, stroking himself, smoking a
    Marlborough
I think of Robert, most afternoons, in a bathhouse,
    in Hollywood

I'm greeted by Randy's hungry wet kisses
I feel his urgent tongue forcing down my throat
I flip his hot body over, grabbing his hairy legs
    tightly
I hoist them angrily into the air, his head buried

in a soft pillow
I enter him forcefully, ignoring his welcoming
        whimpers
I fuck him ruthlessly, punishing him for his
        halting voice mail, thinking I'm his secretary
        in his office, his curt orders I shamelessly
        follow

I grab his hard dick, fucking him, slowly, gently
I feel his tight warmth, fucking him, sturdily,
        steadily
I hear him grunt in pain and sensation, fucking
        him, harder and harder, with abandon
I think about Oscar, wondering how he is, fucking
        him cruelly
I think about why I'm here, why I'm doing this,
        fucking him, feeling weak, feeling close
I think about the countless strangers I've made
        love to in this narrow room, fucking him,
        exploding, biting his neck, screaming
I think about Robert, most afternoons, in a
        bathhouse, in
        Hollywood

I see Randy, walking away, to the sound of roaring
        showers
I wonder if his wife knows about him, me, us
I think about my habit of meeting strangers in
        white towels, in the flickering, dim light of
        my room
I enjoy the welcome anonymity, the immediate

urge to possess these men, to make love to them
I bask in the comfort of their silence, making love
without uttering a word, leaving without a
    sound
I'm always struck by the immediate emptiness and
    disappointment, once the love is made, once the
    door is again shut
I notice how my cavalier, silent lovers seem to
    look like Oscar, how they smell like him, how
    they feel like him
I make love to them the way I made love to Oscar
I wonder if they like me, love me, need me
I wonder if they feel anything for me

I think this, as a nameless man in half light looks
    at me, nodding
I think this, as he drowns me in a sea of hot
    kisses, his fingers, touching me, there
I think this, as he gets on his knees, his head
    against my aching groin, his warm mouth, there
I think this, my head arching back, against a wall,
    my eyes closed
I think of Robert, most afternoons, in a
    bathhouse, in
    Hollywood

Latins Anonymous
Latins Anonymous (Luisa Leschin, Armando Molina, Rick Nájera, Diane Rodríguez)

"Mexican American"

Latins Anonymous is a "comedic analysis of the contemporary Latino condition." Set in a meeting hall and parodying self-help and substance-addiction programs, the characters begin their meeting with their self-introductions: "Hi my name is_____. And I admit I'm a Latino/a." They share the "four H's to live by: We're not Hispanic. We're not Humble. We're not Hostile. We don't Hassle anyone about it. Damn it!" This scene, written by Rick Nájera, is his character's personal testimony.

RICK: I love commercials. They are so educational. They let me know what I need. I got a lot of needs 'cause I'm Mexican-American. Not just Mexican, but American needs. My American side needs football. My Mexican side needs bullfights . . . I know, it's very violent and barbaric, but I love football. I need Mexican food. And American food. My Mexican side needs *carne asada*. My American side needs New York steak, which is basically bland *carne asada*. I love Mexican food. When I see that Rosarita Refried Bean commercial, my Mexican side just wants to take that Rosarita woman and put her on a kitchen table and, wango, wango, wango! and have twelve children through her. But my American side would like to get to know her better, talk to her, establish some honesty, communication, and then wango, wango, wango! And have 2.5 kids with her. My American side would like to hang out with his friends, and that's called a fraternity. But when my Mexican side hangs out with his friends, it's called a street gang! I hate contradictions. I need a world with no contradictions. We all need a world with no contradictions. I call myself Mexican so I won't forget my past, and American because that's what I am. When do I get to call myself an American? When do I get to drive past San Clemente and not get stopped by a guy in a green uniform on top of my trunk looking for illegal aliens. I'm going to say something very controversial. I love *folklórico* dancing. I don't think it's boring at all. Whenever I see a hat in front of me. . . . (*A Mexican hat is thrown in front of him.*) Gotta dance! (*Tries to dance but can't.*) Oh, my God, I've lost my rhythm. My American side is invading my central nervous system. (*In a Mexican voice.*) "You colonizing bastards." (*In a yuppie tone.*) "Go back to Mexico, dude." (*Mexican voice.*) "I din't cross the border. The border crossed me." (*Yuppie voice.*) You foreigner. (*Mexican voice.*) You Gringo. (*Yuppie voice.*) You beaner. (*Mexican voice.*) You Gavacho. (*Yuppie voice.*) You wetback. (*Mexican voice.*) Wetback? Nobody calls me a wetback. I'll kill you. (*He chokes himself. Yuppie voice.*) Help me, help me! The Mexican is going to kill me. Help, help! Somebody call the border patrol!

The Lion and the Jewel
Wole Soyinka

Ilunjinle, a Yoruba Village. The private chamber of Baroka, the Chief. Noon.

Lakunle is the village schoolteacher, Western-educated and nearly twenty-three. "He is dressed in an old-style English suit, threadbare but not ragged, clean but not ironed, obviously a size or two too small. . . ." He is in love with Sidi, "the village belle," who flirts with him freely, but mocks him for his resistance to traditional ways and deplores his rejection of the bride-price, a prerequisite to her consent to marriage. Lakunle calls it a "savage custom, barbaric, out-dated, rejected, denounced, accursed, excommunicated, archaic, degrading, humiliating, unspeakable, redundant. Retrogressive, remarkable, unpalatable." Sidi teases, "Is the bag empty? Why did you stop?" to which Lakunle rejoins, "I own only the *Shorter Companion Dictionary*, but I have ordered *The Longer One*—you wait!"

The village is buzzing with the second appearance of "the stranger," a photographer who has returned with a magazine which features the village and pictures of Sidi, confirming her extraordinary beauty and inflating her sense of self. The magazine comes to the attention of Baroka, "the Bale of Ilunjinle," He is sixty-two: Admiring the magazine he muses, "Yes, yes . . . it is five full months since last I took a wife . . . five full months." But it is more than Sidi's beauty that motivates him as he has recently found himself unable to perform with his favorite wife. He summons his First Wife, Sadiku, and confides in her his real reason for seeking Sidi as his bride.

BAROKA: The time has come when I can fool myself
No more. I am no man, Sadiku. My manhood
Ended near a week ago.
I wanted Sidi because I still hoped—
A foolish thought I know, but still—I hoped
That, with a virgin young and hot within,
My failing strength would rise and save my pride.
(SADIKU *begins to moan.*)
A waste of hope. I knew it even then.
But it's a human failing never to accept
The worst; and so I pandered to my vanity.
When manhood must, it ends.
The well of living, tapped beyond its depth,
Dries up, and mocks the wastrel in the end.
I am withered and unsapped, the joy
Of ballad-mongers, the aged butt
Of youth's ribaldry.
(As if suddenly aware of her presence, BAROKA starts up.)
I have told this to no one but you,
Who are my eldest, my most faithful wife.
But if you dare parade my shame before the world . . .
(SADIKU *shakes her head in protest and begins to stroke the soles of
his feet with renewed tenderness.* BAROKA *sighs and falls back slowly.*)
How irritable I have grown of late
Such doubts to harbour of your loyalty . . .
But this disaster is too much for one
Checked thus as I upon the prime of youth.
That rains that blessed me from my birth
Number a meagre sixty-two;
While my grandfather, that man of teak,
Fathered two sons, late on sixty-five.

But Okiki, my father beat them all
Producing female twins at sixty-seven.
Why then must I, descendant of these lions
Forswear my wives at a youthful sixty-two
My veins of life run dry, my manhood gone!
(*His voice goes drowsy;* SADIKU *sighs and moans and
caresses his feet. His face lights up suddenly with rapture.*)
Sango bear witness! These weary feet
Have felt the loving hands of much design
In women.
My soles have felt the scratch of harsh,
Gravelled hands.
They have borne the heaviness of clumsy,
Gorilla paws.
And I have known the tease of tiny,
Dainty hands,
Toy-like hands that tantalized
My eager senses,
Promised of thrills to come
Remaining
Unfulfilled because the fingers
Were too frail,
The touch too light and faint to pierce
The incredible thickness of my soles.
But thou Sadiku, thy plain unadorned hands
Encase a sweet sensuality which age
Will not destroy. A-ah,
Oyayi! Beyond a doubt Sadiku,
Thou art the queen of them all.
(*Falls asleep.*)

The Lion and the Jewel
Wole Soyinka

The Village Center. Night.

Lakunle comes upon Sadiku the First Wife and Sidi, dancing derisively around "a carved figure of the Bale, naked and in full detail." Sadiku has told Sidi of the chief's impotence, and the two are plotting to humiliate him. Lakunle is aghast and begs Sidi not to go to Baroka: "If you care one little bit for what I feel, do not go to torment the man. . . ." Sadiku turns to mock Lakunle, "The bride-price, is that paid. . . ? Why don't you do what other men have done. Take a farm for a season. . . . Or will the smell of the wet soil be too much for your delicate nostrils?" With conviction, Lakunle details the changes he is certain are coming to the village.

LAKUNLE (*with conviction*): Within a year or two, I swear,
This town shall see a transformation
Bride-price will be a thing forgotten
And wives shall take their place by men.
A motor road will pass this spot
And bring the city ways to us.
We'll buy saucepans for all the women
Clay pots are crude and unhygienic
No man shall take more wives than one

That's why they're impotent too soon.
The ruler shall ride cars, not horses
Or a bicycle at the very least.
We'll burn the forest, cut the trees
Then plant a modern park for lovers
We'll print newspapers every day
With pictures of seductive girls.
The world will judge our progress by
The girls that win beauty contests.
While Lagos builds new factories daily
We only play 'ayo' and gossip.
Where is our school of ballroom dancing?
Who here can throw a cocktail party?
We must be modern with the rest
Or live forgotten by the world
We must reject the palm wine habit
And take to tea, with milk and sugar.
(*Turns on* SADIKU, *who has been staring at him in terror. She retreats,
and he continues to talk down at her as they go round, then down and
offstage,* LAKUNLE*'s hectoring voice trailing away in the distance.*)
This is my plan, you withered face
And I shall start by teaching you.
From now you shall attend my school
And take your place with twelve-year-olds.
For though you're nearly seventy,
Your mind is simple and unformed.
Have you no shame that at your age,
You neither read nor write nor think?
You spend your days as senior wife,
Collecting brides for Baroka.
And now because you've sucked him dry,
  You send my Sidi to his shame. . . .

Ma Rainey's Black Bottom
August Wilson

Act I. A recording studio in Chicago. Early March, 1927.

Levee is a musician, a cornet player, in Ma Rainey's band. He is waiting for the temperamental singer to show up for a recording session. Talented and easily provoked, Levee sets himself apart from the other musicians, scoffing at their "old jug-band music." He is writing music that he hopes to record ("I'm talking about art! . . . I'm gonna get me a band and make me some records"). He annoys his fellow band members, chiding them about their musicianship. He refuses to rehearse with them ("What's the point in it?"). He informs them that the producer is interested in his music. ("I done give Mr. Sturdyvant some of my songs I wrote and he say he's gonna let me record them when I get my band together"). His mood grows increasingly antagonistic as he asserts both his individuality and superiority to his peers, leading the others to comment, "I don't know why you waste your time on this fool," and, "Levee, you ain't nothing but the devil."

When Ma Rainey finally arrives she refuses to record Levee's arrangements: "I ain't studying Levee nothing. I know what he done to that song and I don't like to sing it that way. I'm doing it the old way. . . ." The producer acquiesces to her, and Levee is bitterly disappointed. When the producer tells Levee that he is still interested in seeing Levee's songs, he answers eagerly: "Yessir! As soon as you get the chance, Mr. Sturdyvant." The other musicians mock Levee: "You heard this nigger. . . . Shuffling them feet. . . . Spooked up by the white man." Levee turns on them angrily.

LEVEE: Levee got to be Levee! And he don't need nobody messing with him about the white man—'cause you don't know nothing about me. You don't know Levee. You don't know nothing about what kind of blood I got! What kind of heart I got beating here! I was eight years old when I watched a gang of white mens come into my daddy's house and have to do with my mama anyway they wanted. Never will forget it.

We was living in Jefferson County, about eighty miles outside of Natchez. My daddy's name was Memphis . . . Memphis Lee Green . . . had him near fifty acres of good farming land. I'm talking good land! Grow anything you want! He done gone off of shares and bought this land from Mr. Hallie's widow-woman after he done passed on. Folks called him an uppity nigger 'cause he done saved and borrowed to where he could buy this land and be independent.

It was coming on planting time and my daddy went into Natchez to get him some seed and fertilizer. Called me, say, Levee, you the man of the house now. Take care of your mama while I'm gone. I wasn't but a little boy, eight years old.

My mama was frying up some chicken when them mens come in that house. Must have been eight or nine of them. She was standing there frying that chicken and them mens come and took hold of her just like you take hold of a mule and make him do what you want.

There was my mama with a gang of white mens. She tried to fight them off, but I could see where it wasn't gonna do her any good. I didn't know what they were doing to her . . . but I figured whatever it was they may as well do to me, too. My daddy had a knife that he kept around there for hunting and working and whatnot. I knew where he kept it and I went and got it. (*Crosses to bench and puts his cornet on it.*) I'm gonna show you how spooked up I was by the white man. I tried my damnedest to cut one of them's throat! I hit

102

him on the shoulder with it. (*Crosses to other bench.*) He reached back and grabbed hold of that knife and whacked me across the chest with it. (*Pulls up his shirt and exposes a long, ugly scar on his chest.*) That's what made them stop. They was scared I was gonna bleed to death. My mama wrapped a sheet around me and carried me two miles down to the Furlow place and they drove me up to Doc Albans. He was waiting on a calf to be born and said he ain't had time to see me. They carried me up to Miss Etta, the midwife, and she fixed me up.

My daddy came back and acted like he done accepted the facts of what happened. But he got the names of them white men from my mama. He found out who they was and then we announced we was moving out of the county. Said good-bye to everybody . . . all the neighbors. My daddy went and smiled in the face of one of them crackers who had been with my mama. Smiled in his face and sold him our land. We moved over with relations in Caldwell. He got us settled in and then he took off one day. I ain't never seen him since. He sneaked back hiding up in the woods, laying to get them eight or nine men.

He got four of them before they got him. They tracked him down in the woods. Caught up with him, hung him, and set him afire. (*Turns to the silver cornet on the bench.*) My daddy wasn't spooked up by the white man. Nosir! And that taught me how to handle them. (*Slowly crosses to the cornet, lifts it, and clutches it tightly to his chest, grief-stricken.*) I seen my daddy go up and grin in this cracker's face . . . smile in his face, and sell him his land. All the while he's planning how he's gonna get him and what he's gonna do to him. That taught me how to handle them. So you all just back up and leave Levee alone about the white man. I can smile and say "yessir" to whoever I please. (*Crosses to the other bench, subdued.*) I got my time coming to me. You all just leave Levee alone about the white man.

The Meeting
Jeff Stetson

Act 1. Scene 1. A hotel room in Harlem. February 14, 1965.

The Meeting is about a fictionalized encounter between civil rights leader
Dr. Martin Luther King and black nationalist leader Malcolm X. King has
come, at Malcolm's invitation, to Malcolm's hotel room the afternoon
Malcolm's home has been firebombed. The two engage in a tense discussion in which Malcolm pushes King to see the error in his pacifist
approach: "Your unity is sitting around the camp fire while the cross is
burning singing, 'we shall overcome'. . . . If you're really for unity you'd be
singing, 'we shall come over!'. . . We can't learn from martyrs anymore,
Martin. . . . You want to be able to buy a cup of coffee . . . I want us to be
able to sell it. . . ." King explains his commitment to nonviolence: "Do you
think that it is easy for me to see our own people beaten? . . . I don't preach
nonviolence because I like it! I preach it because it's right. And, because
I'm a man. And because I'm a child of God!" Having reached an impasse,
they both decide further discussion is futile. Before he leaves, King gives
Malcolm a paper bag containing a toy doll, a gift from his daughter,
Yolanda, to Malcolm's daughter, Atallah. Softening, the men speak about
their families and personal losses. When Malcolm allows himself to think
about the sacrifice his family has made ("I have nothing to leave my own
family, no more money, now not even a home. . . . And yet, I still wonder,
was there more I should have done . . . more of myself I could give?") King
responds with a story.

105

Dr. King: My father used to tell me the story of a young Baptist minister who had gone North to seek his fame and fortune. After he had become very successful, the pastor of his former small southern church extended an invitation to return home for a visit and preach before his old congregation. Well, this minister could hardly refuse such an offer, in fact, he was rather proud at the thought of coming back and showin' the folk how successful he had become. He decided to bring his seven-year-old son with him, to teach him a lesson about his history . . . his roots. . . . When the minister returned to his old church he was moved so much that he proceeded to give one of the best sermons of his life . . . had the congregation rollin' from one emotion to another. When it was all over the Pastor threw his arms around the young minister and said: "John, that was a truly moving and inspirational sermon . . . I wish we could give you some kind of honorarium, but as you know, our church is not doing so well." (*Both* Malcolm *and* King *laugh.*) John just waved the Pastor off and said that was fine, it was payment enough simply to return home for a visit. As John and his son were leaving, they passed the church collection box. John stopped and took out a crisp new ten-dollar bill and placed it in the box. He and his son then proceeded out of the church to the parking lot. As they were getting into the car all of a sudden the Pastor came running outside calling John's name. As the Pastor caught up to John he said: "I know you don't want any payment, but we just couldn't let you leave without at least a token of our appreciation." The Pastor handed John a crisp new ten-dollar bill which John immediately recognized as the one he placed in the collection box, just moments before. He took the money, exchanged final farewells with the Pastor and got into his car. After a moment or two, he looked at his son, smiling proudly and confidently and said: "Son, I hope this teaches you a lesson." His son nodded, looked at his father and said: "Yes Dad, it has. If you had given more, you would have gotten more." (MALCOLM *laughs, but* DR. KING *smiles sadly. He gives a quiet and distant look, then softly to* MALCOLM *he says:*) We all have to give more, Malcolm. . . . More than we thought we needed to. Even then, sometimes it's not enough.

Men on the Verge of a His-panic Breakdown
Guillermo Reyes

"Goodbye to Sugar Daddy"

Guillermo Reyes's solo performance piece gives us a "gallery of gay Hispanic men" who are survivors of "transcultural shock." In "Goodbye to Sugar Daddy," we meet Vinnie, "an anal-retentive-looking man, 30. He was once a very pretty younger man." His white, older partner has just dumped him for a younger lover.

VINNIE: (*to unseen man*)
He's 18? . . . No, no bother.

The point is well taken, Sugar Daddy. Don't worry, it doesn't take me that long to pack. I can be out of here in a matter of minutes.

Now, if you could just sign here, and here, and down here. . . . This form will help me seek compensation from the Society of West Hollywood Kept Boys over 30. . . . Please, say no more. You'll be late for the Gay Republican fund-raiser.

I am *not* upset. Please. Let's be businesslike about this. And I'll leave a receipt for your taxes, yes. . . . Don't worry about me. I've been meaning to visit the folks back in Colombia, the ones who survived the last volcano eruption. I've got all the bases covered. Self-reliant, independent, one-man show—that's me. Oh, I'll leave written instructions for the new eighteen-year-old from Wichita, Kansas, so he can deal with your prostate gland medicine.

You'll be late. . . . Good-bye, Sugar Daddy.

(*He watches* Sugar Daddy *go. A halfhearted wave good-bye. . . . He's left alone. He looks around the room. He lights a cigarette. He makes a phone call.*)

Hello, is this Lenny? Lenny, darling, how are you? Nice to hear your voice again after all these years. Why it's Vinnie. Vinnie Contreras. Oh, come now. . . . I was twenty; you were twenty-nine. Ten years or so ago, remember?

I came in clutching Sugar Daddy's arm, and we kindly asked you to depart from our presence. Yes, I helped you pack. But no, I don't remember throwing your bags out the window. Let memory be more selective, Lenny! Lenny?!? . . . So what have you been doing with your life? What? Oh, no particular reason, just wanted to keep in touch. No, no, it's not that at all—alright, Lenny, he's eighteen; he's blond, fresh from Kansas. What am I to do, Lenny? Oh, oh, Lenny. . . .

But please let me ask you, and I hope it's not too personal. What did you do after you voluntarily departed from Sugar Daddy's presence? . . . How many years at the shelter? I can't stand poor lighting, you know. But okay, afterwards, what did you do afterwards? Dry cleaning? . . . Oh, I love dry cleaning, you know. I love the hangers and the plastic wrap that makes the clothes look so, you know, pressed! So how much do they pay? . . . Oh, well, that's just slightly below the minimum wage. . . . And no health care—well, that would be too Hillary, wouldn't it?

Listen, Lenny, do you think there might be an opening at the dry cleaners anytime soon? No, I just figured at this time in my life I could use some . . . some flexibility. I'm exploring different venues for making a living. I'd like to be open to career alternatives. . . . So, when do you think there might be an opening? Soon, you said? Oh, you didn't say.

Well, you'll keep me in mind, won't you, Lenny? Oh, no, no, Colombia is not for me these days, you know. I'm not sure if I belong at home at all, you know. No, I couldn't. I couldn't go back. I burned too many bridges. Literally. . . . Too many people tend to die when I burn bridges. . . .

Lenny, wait! One more thing—

How did you ever feel about Sugar Daddy? You know, feelings. As in emotion? I know that about a half century separates me from him, but it can happen, right? Can it happen that after so many years, you begin to feel a certain attachment to the creature? Oh, Lenny, there comes a time when even people like us develop feelings, don't you think? . . . No, I'm not—I'm not crazy, Lenny. After awhile, you begin to develop feelings for those who pay your rent, feelings as noble and complex as any others. Feelings for his loose skin against your thighs, his dentures stuck in your pubic hair, his cancer-ridden lungs breathing sweet warm air against your face.

Yes, Lenny, I love Sugar Daddy. I love Sugar Daddy! Only now do I realize it. Only now have I come to that conclusion. Please don't. Don't hang up! . . . [*Desperate to keep him on the phone*] We must get together for cappuccino in West Hollywood. Tea at Trumps? Attitude at the Studio? You no longer "do" attitude? Lenny!

(*He hangs up the phone. He grabs his suitcase and holds it in his arms as a barrier against the world before him.*)

Well, I suppose I understand why you had to hang up. I am alone now, ready to hit the streets. So here I go. . . . I am one of the few, one of the brave, one of the Aging Kept Boys of West Hollywood.

I am not afraid. You hear that, world? (*As he "clicks his heels" three times*)

I am not afraid. I am not afraid. I AM NOT AFRAID!

(*Lights fade out.*)

The Mighty Gents
Richard Wesley

Scene 1. The streets of Newark, New Jersey. The 1970s.

Frankie, age thirty, is the leader of the Mighty Gents, an aging street gang living on its past glory. Frankie is a natural leader who has enjoyed the street life, but is now facing a crossroads. His home life is tense because he and his girlfriend, Rita, have been unable to have a baby. Striving to keep his reputation on the streets, he is troubled by a recurring nightmare: "In the dream I'm alone and surrounded by wolves." Unable to let go of the past he asserts, "I was one of the baddest dudes who ever walked the streets of this city." His girlfriend Rita, responds, "Yea. You *was* a lotta things, Frankie." The play opens with this monologue, in which Frankie details an incident that moved him to the life he has chosen.

FRANKIE: Once, when I was about fifteen, I met this broad who was around thirty at the time. I was young an' tryin' to be fly and the mysteries of sex still held a certain kind fascination for me. I usedta think that sex with a older woman would make me a man much quicker. The older guys on the block always usedta say that this broad really had it together when it came to gettin' down. I wanted to be more experienced like those guys. I didn't wanna be an ignorant chump alla my life. One day she came up to me an' the next thing I knew I was goin' up to her apartment. We sat down to talk an' listen to some jazz. She taught me about Charlie Parker, Billie Holliday, and Bud Powell—people I had never heard of before. I was really gettin' my mind completely blown. Here I was, bein' made to appreciate some music you couldn't even dance to. She served me this dynamite wine and told me about places she'd been to—places I'd only seen on TV. I really dug her rap. I was learning so much. I just knew this was gonna be my night. We drank some more and then she gave me the first joint I ever smoked. We all were wineheads in those days so a joint was really exotic. It was from Mexico. Outa sight. Then, there was no longer anything to talk about. We both knew why I was there, but she didn't treat me like I was a stud or somethin'. I really dug not bein' made fun of or used 'cause I was young. Yea, so we went into the bedroom an' she told me to lie down on the bed. Then she started to undress me an' when I was naked she took this oil an' began to massage me all over and hummed this tune. She kept tellin' me how beautiful I was. None of the girls I knew could do the things she was doin' to me with her voice and her hands. Hey man, I was hooked. I thought to myself that the only thing a young girl could do for me was lead me to a grown woman. So, I just lay there tryin' to be cool. You know, talkin' outa the side of my mouth, tryin' to be profound, hopin' she wouldn't see how nervous I was. I had to really concentrate to keep from gettin' an erection. Didn't want her to think I was weak emotionally. You know? Then, she started to get undressed. I wanted to watch but I turned my head 'cause I didn't want her to think I wasn't used to seein' a nekked woman. Soon, she was finished an' she came toward the bed. And then I knew why everything was goin' so well: "She" was more well-hung than I was. I wanted to run but I couldn't. I wanted to bust that freak in his mouth, but I was afraid I might get killed. So, I just lay there and let him do whatever he wanted to. I was there a coupla hours. Seemed like I was never

114

gonna leave. Then, finally I was gone. When I got in the street I threw up. I slept in an alleyway 'cause I was too ashamed to go home. I don't remember much of anything else from that entire month except that I screwed every girl I could and did everything that was considered manly, extra hard. Anything to prove to myself that I wasn't a . . . well, you know. Yah, then I joined the Mighty Gents an' started a lucrative career as a head-knocker. After I drew first blood against the Zombies, I didn't doubt myself ever again. That freak died of a drug overdose five years ago. I wonder if he ever thought about me.

Miriam's Flowers
Migdalia Cruz

Scene 8. At Puli's gravestone in a cemetary in the South Bronx. 1975.

Nando Morales is a thirty-seven-year-old Puerto Rican man whose seven-year-old son, Puli, was killed while chasing a baseball across the train tracks. His arm was never found; when he was buried, "They had to pin up his sleeve like a little cripple boy in his little box . . . small and white, like a little bathtub." Puli's sister, Miriam, his mother, Delfina, and Nando are all struggling with the fact of his death. Puli loved baseball and ". . . always wanned to be in the paper like . . . Roberto Clemente." His death was published in the newspaper, showing him how he was. All in pieces . . . the first one of us ever been in the paper. . . ." After the funeral, Nando visits his son's grave. He "whistles a Spanish children's song as he bounces a baseball off the side of Puli's gravestone. . . ."

NANDO: Men have to work. You can't be home all the time when you're a man. You unnerstan' me? (*Pause.*) And . . . and I taught you the same. When you're the man of the house, you work. I work. I know you unnerstan'. Women don't unnerstan'. They expect you to be there all the time, watching over everything. I can't be in two places at the same time, Puli. I know you know that. I'm not no fockin' magician. (*Pause.*) And it's a good job I have for the kind of brain I got. I can always remember numbers. That's important in a post office . . . I put numbers together in my head and they come out like a picture. Like the number seven, I see it and it's a big wooden arrow pointing out. (*Pause.*) So . . . when you got a family, you make money. You watch out for your sisters. And you don't let nobody look at your wife. You don't let other men look at what's yours. You . . . take care of it. (*Pause.*) Men don't get scared. Not of other men. If you get scared of other men, you hide it. It helps if you hit them . . . yeah, when you feel their bones cracked against your fist, that's a good feeling. We keep it under control. My papi used to tell me that the only people you respect are the people who can beat you. . . . (*He bounces the ball off the gravestone in silence.*) Puerto Ricans are good at baseball. That's another thing women don't unnerstan'. If you play good baseball, you can be good at everything else because nothing else means anything . . . I wasn't ever really good at it, but my papi wanned me to be. I know he did because he beat the shit outta me whenever I missed a catch. He tole me only faggots like carving things outta wood. Men play sports. And that's right. You don' get nowhere making things. I mean, if you wanned to make things, I woulda let you, but that's because you got a great arm. When you're good at baseball, people leave you alone. (*Pause.*) People woulda loved you, Puli. You woulda been something. (*Fade out.*)

The Mojo and the Sayso
Aishah Rahman

Act 1. The living room of the Benjamins' home. Now. Sunday. Morning.

It's been three years since the death of ten-year-old Linus Benjamin, who was shot by the police in a case of mistaken identity. The check compensating his family for "Payment of Wrongful Death" has just arrived. Since Linus's death, his father, Acts, has immersed himself in building a car in the middle of the living room: "Soon I'll be finished [with] the dream car of my mind." Awilda, his wife, readies herself to go to church alone, as usual, and frets over the check: "How do they add up what a ten-year-old boy's life is worth to his parents?" Their older son, Walter, has changed dramatically since his brother's death; Awilda laments, "He was smart! He was kind! He was tender! . . . Now he's got a grenade for a soul. . . ." Walter has changed his name to Blood; he enters the house brandishing a gun and is disarmed by Acts. Acts admonishes him by saying, "Don't let what happened to Linus madden or cheapen you. I bear a lot of pain but I bear it with expression. Just who in the hell do you think you are?" Blood then expresses his new identity.

BLOOD (*Walks away from him*): Who am I? I want to be a righteous gunman like George Jackson. Or his brother, Jonathan. I would have liked to walk in the courtroom where they acquitted the cop that shot my brother in the back with my guns drawn and announce, "All right, gentlemen, I'm taking over." Just like Jonathan did. Alone and armed. Righteous and tough. Beyond fear. He knew his fate and did not hesitate. A man evolved to the highest level. Now they mighta shot some bullets into Jonathan Jackson's brain that day but he ain't dead. I got to be him 'cause I sure ain't me. I should be the kind of man that pours down hot revenge on his enemies because I had a brother, once. A kid brother. Sometimes he used to pee in the bed. A scrawny, ash-brown kid, ninety-four pounds, about this high. He was always beating up on little girls 'cause he liked them. Used to be afraid of being weak and afraid. We used to armwrestle all the time and I'd let him win and then show him how I could beat him anytime I wanted to. He looked up to me and I liked that.

The Mojo and the Sayso
Aishah Rahman

Act 2. Scene 2. The living room of the Benjamins' home. Now. Sunday.
Evening.

Awilda returns from church accompanied by the Pastor; she has decided
to give the check to the church in Linus's name. When the Pastor is
revealed as a "dandy man" preying on his congregation, Acts, Awilda, and
Blood drive him from their home. Before tearing the check to shreds, Acts
for the first time tells his family what actually happened on the day of the
fatal shooting.

Acts: It's funny how it always comes back to money. It's funny how
money is supposed to explain everything and make anything all
right. It was a Saturday, right before dawn, and as you know, the boy
and I were on our way to the yard. Fooling around with cars is in my
bones so I figure since Linus takes after me in so many ways he
could learn it real good and earn a little change too. So when he
turned ten, he started coming with me on Saturday mornings 'cause
the rest of the week he's in school like he's supposed to be. He was
a nice boy. Very respectful. Very intelligent. He would have been a
good mechanic some day.

I remember it was early spring but the dew made it cold. The sky was that light purplish gray you get right before dawn. We was both walking, not saying too much. I guess it was just too early to be doing a lot of talking. We walked down New York Boulevard through the vacant lot littered with broken glass, past the trees that rise right out of the trash and grow fifty feet tall. Suddenly two guys with plain clothes pull up in a plain car and yell at us, "Stop." Their car screams to a halt. I didn't even recognize them as humans so how should I know they was cops, creeping toward us, hissing, "Stop, you sons of bitches," laughing and drinking as they cursed us. Said in the papers they was looking for two grown burglars. My little son and I wasn't no burglars.

My wallet was bulging on my hip. I had just gotten paid. I had it all figured out. These drunken jokers are ordinary crooks trying to rob me. I figure the way they are drinking I can outrun both of them and you remember how Linus could outrun a chicken. "Run," I command and we take off. Linus shoots out in front of me and I was right behind.

They didn't even chase us. A flat loud sound ripped the air and Linus fell and instantly became a red pool, his eyes a bright, white blank. They shot Linus in the back. They killed him! They shot my boy!

Always, always, in my head, "Should I have stood my ground and fought them? Was I trying to protect my money more than Linus?" Ain't no way I could run away and leave Linus alone, is there? LINUS RAN AHEAD OF ME AND LEFT ME! I know that's the way it happened. But sometimes a man can get confused and the way something awful happens isn't always the way you remember it. I play it back all the time in my head and my only thought that night was to protect Linus. At least that's the way I remember it.

Night of the Assassins
José Triana

Act 2. A basement or an attic. The 1950s.

Lalo, thirty years old, and his two sisters are "adults, but exhibit a fading adolescent grace" like "figures in a ruined museum." They are left together in a room reenacting roles for each other as they explore the possible consequences of imaginary actions. "In this house, everything is a part of the game"; what's at stake is "the salvation of your souls." The house is a "labyrinth" which "has systematically obstructed all attempts to arrive at the truth." Stuck in the midst of this seemingly inescapable maze, Lalo has become "indifferent, relaxed, immune to any feelings of tenderness, understanding, or pity." This numbness allows him to play the part of an assassin for his sisters and be tried by them for the attempted murder of his parents. This play has been seen by many as an allegory for prerevolutionary Cuban society.

Lalo: It's true. I got used to it. (*As* Lalo *progresses through the monologue, he becomes transformed*). It sounds terrible, but . . . It's not how I wanted it, but the idea kept on buzzing around in my head. At first, I wanted it to go away. Do you know what I mean? But it kept on telling me: "Kill your parents. Kill your parents." I thought I was going crazy, I swear. I jumped into bed. I started getting the shivers

. . . I had a temperature. I thought I would pop like a balloon. I thought the devil was beckoning to me. I lay trembling under the blankets . . . You should have seen me . . . I couldn't sleep. Not a wink night after night. It was dreadful. I saw death creeping up on me from behind the bed, from between the curtains, from inside the wardrobe. It became my shadow and whispered to me from inside the pillows: "Assassin." And then, as if by magic, it disappeared. And I sat in front of the mirror and saw my mother lying dead in her coffin and my father hanging by his neck laughing and shouting at me. And at night I felt my mother's hands in the pillows, scratching my face. (*Pause.*) Every morning I woke up in pain. It was as if I were rising from the dead, clasped by two corpses which had been chasing me in my dreams. There were moments when I was tempted . . . but no . . . no . . . Leave home? No way! I knew what I was up against . . . I would always come back and then I would promise never to do it again. By then I was determined never again to embark on that crazy adventure. Anything but that! Then I had the idea of arranging the house in my own way, of running things myself. . . . The living room is not the living room, I said to myself. The living room is the kitchen. The bedroom is not the bedroom. The bedroom is the bathroom. (*Short pause.*) What else could I do? If I didn't do that, I would end up destroying everything. Everything. Because everything was complicit, everything was plotting against me; everything knew my every thought. If I sat down in a chair, the chair wasn't the chair but my father's corpse. If I picked up a glass of water, I felt that what I had in my hands was my dead mother's damp neck. If I played with a vase, an enormous knife would suddenly fall out of it. If I cleaned the carpets, I could never finish the job because they turned into an enormous clot of blood. (*Pause.*) Haven't you ever felt like that? I was suffocating, suffocating. I didn't know where I was or what it was all about. And who could I talk to? Was there anyone I could trust? I was stuck in a deep hole and there was no way out. . . . (*Pause.*) But I had a strange idea that I could save myself. . . . I don't know what from. . . . Anyway, it's just an expression. . . . You try to explain the whole thing and you almost . . . usually you can't. . . . Perhaps I wanted to save myself from the suffocating, from being shut in. . . . Soon after, without knowing why, things began to change. I heard a voice one day, but I didn't know where it was coming from. . . . And then I heard my sisters laughing and joking all round the house. And mixed in with their laughter I heard thousands of voices repeating in unison: "Kill them. Kill them." No, I'm not just making it up. I swear it's true. (*As if inspired.*) From then on I knew what I had to do. Gradually I realised that everything, the carpets, the bed, the wardrobes, the mirror, the vases, the glasses, the spoons and my own shadow, they were all murmuring, telling me: "Kill your parents." (*He says it in an almost musical ecstasy.*) "Kill your parents." The whole house, everything, everything was pushing me towards this heroic act. (*Pause.*)

Paper Angels
Genny Lim

Scene 8. The men's dormitory of the Angel Island Immigration and Detention Center, San Francisco Harbor, 1915.

Chin Gung is a Chinese sojourner to the United States, "an old timer, with a taste for freedom and adventure who's been in the United States long enough to cultivate American habits, but who's never lost his traditional Chinese values and outlook on life." The play is set during a time when racist immigration laws severely restricted the movement of Chinese to the United States and prospective immigrants were held for long periods of time—months and even years—on Angel Island in the San Francisco harbor while being subjected to grueling interviews. Passing the time in the men's dormitory, separated from the Chinese wife he has brought across an ocean after forty years, Chin Gung speaks about his life in America and the long-anticipated "homecoming" with his wife.

CHIN GUNG: Everybody says Ol' Chin is crazy. I've moved all around this country. After the rails, we followed the seasons—like geese, always looking for better climate, better conditions. I've picked lemons and artichoke. I've harvested walnuts with long poles and caught the falling nuts with sacks. I was a good cook so when the cook ran off, 'cause he couldn't pay off his gambling debt, I had to prepare the meals for thirty, sometimes as many as fifty men a day. I got so frustrated with my life, I gambled away all my earnings one day. The more desperate you are, the crazier you get. (*Pauses.*) I'll tell you one thing though, I know this land, I ache for her sometimes, like she was my woman. When I dig my hands into her flesh and seed her, something grows; when I water and fertilize her, she begins to swell. If you treat her with respect, she responds, just like a woman. A lot of whites don't know this. (*Pauses.*) You probably think I'm crazy, but I'm in love with this land. I want to die in America.

(LUM: Not me. As soon as I strike it rich, I'm taking the first boat back home.)

CHIN GUNG: I went to all this trouble bringing my wife with me this time. She waited forty years for me. Imagine that? Forty years. I figure she deserves something better than staring at the backside of a pig all her life. She's no young girl anymore. No, now she's a grandma and I'm a grandpa, except we got no grandchildren. That's not right, you know? Old people should have grandchildren. That way something of them lives on after they're gone. As for me, it's too late. (*Reminisces.*) Some of those sing-song girls were pretty nice. Especially Lilly. I could have married her. But how could I do that to my China wife, huh?

Roosters
Milcha Sanchez-Scott

Act Two. Scene 1. The Southwest. The present.

Hector Morales is a handsome young man, about twenty. His father is the legendary Gallo, a master cockfighter who has just been released from prison, having served time for manslaughter. In Gallo's absence, Hector has become a farm laborer, the first Morales to go into the fields. Hector's grandfather, Abuelo, gave him the rooster, Zapata, before his death, rather than give it to his son, Gallo. Although the rest of the family is anticipating Gallo's return home with excitement, Hector is indifferent: "He was never here for us, never a card, a little present for Angela. He forgot us. . . . Just make it clear to him. Abuelo left the bird to me, not to him, to me."

Hector's reunion with Gallo is strained; Gallo immediately offers advice about the handling of Zapata: "Let him out . . . he needs a bigger carrier . . . he's a flyer." Coaxing Hector to take the bird out, he reminds Hector of the first time he witnessed a cockfight, as Hector reminisces.

HECTOR (*to himself*): It was in Jacinto Park . . . the crowd was a monster, made up of individual human beings stuck together by sweat and spittle. Their gaping mouths let out screams, curses, and foul gases, masticating, smacking, eager for the kill. You stood up. The monster roared. Quasimoto, your bird, in one hand. You lifted him high, "Pit!" went the call. "Pit!" roared the monster. And you threw him into the ring . . . soaring with the blades on his heels flashing. I heard the mighty rage of his wings and my heart soared with him. He was a whirlwind flashing and slashing like a dark avenging angel then like some distant rainbow star exploding he was hit. The monster crowd inhaled, sucking back their hopes . . . in that vacuum he was pulled down. My heart went down the same dark shaft, my brains slammed against the earth's hard crust . . . my eyes clouded . . . my arteries gushed . . . my lungs collapsed. "Get up," said Abuelo, "up here with me, and you will see a miracle." You, Father, picked up Quasimoto, a lifeless pile of bloody feathers, holding his head oh so gently, you closed your eyes, and like a great wave receding, you drew a breath that came from deep within your ocean floor. I heard the stones rumble, the mountains shift, the topsoil move, and as your breath slammed on the beaches, Quasimoto sputtered back to life. Oh Papi, breathe on me.

The Talented Tenth
Richard Wesley

Act 1. Scene 2. A beach in Jamaica. The early 1990s.

At the beginning of the play, Bernard is a Howard University graduate who
wants to be a "success" but has "no concrete plan in place" of how to
reach this general goal. At his first job interview in America, he is told by
an African American executive that "no individual in this country is more
powerful than the ethnic group from which he comes" and that "the primary arena in which our people's struggle must be won . . . is Economics,"
not civil rights. He puts his faith in the idea that he has "no rights, no
privileges, no nothing" and that his "job as a Negro businessman is to
make money, be successful and be a springboard for whatever is to follow."
Years later, Bernard thinks to himself, "I was once twenty-two, fresh out
of college, with an unlimited horizon in front of me. Then, just like that, I
was twenty-five, then suddenly thirty, then forty-three . . . I want to change
my life. . . . But I don't dare ACT. And yet, I WANT to act . . . I've got to
act . . . before it's too late." In this monologue he compares his experience
in college to the present.

Lights up on BERNARD, *alone, putting a sweatsuit on over his beachwear.*

BERNARD: It was during my junior year in college. Martin Luther King
tried to lead a march across the Edmund Pettus Bridge in Selma,

Alabama, but the local authorities had a law against it. Those were the days down South when there were laws against black people doing anything, including being black, if you get my drift. Well, Dr. King decided to march anyway, and the sheriff's people attacked the marchers and threw them in jail. People all over the country called on President Johnson to do something, but Johnson hesitated. Then, Dr. King announced he would march again, this time all the way to Montgomery, the state capital. The Klan started making noises. And Lyndon Johnson still hesitated. So, the Student Nonviolent Coordinating Committee went into action. They had a local chapter down on Rhode Island Avenue, not that far from the campus, and Habiba and I went down there right after philosophy class and signed up together. We were ready, y'all.

I remember my heart was beating a mile a minute. The both of us were so excited. We were finally in the big fight: helping the Race in the Civil Rights Struggle. We were active participants in making History.

The room was filled with nervous energy. People sang civil rights songs and hugged each other and held hands—men and women, black and white.

Then came speeches and pronouncements to get us fired up. Lots of fists clenched in the air. The room was hot and sweaty and filled with cigarette smoke. I felt a little dizzy and reached for Habiba. Someone began singing, "Precious Lord Take My Hand," and folks joined in. We all held hands and closed our eyes and let the power of the song take hold of us. Then, Habiba started shaking, gasping for breath, like she was convulsing. Suddenly, she opened her eyes and looked at me, saying she'd had a race memory. She was with a group of runaway slaves. Armed gunmen had chased them through a swamp. They were trapped with no way out. They began to sing, calling out to God, and the more they sang, the stronger they became. She saw the flash of the gunfire. She felt the bullets searing into her flesh. But she kept getting stronger. They all kept getting stronger. Then, Habiba screamed. Just like that. A scream like I'd never heard before. Everyone in the room just stopped. It was like we all felt what she felt. People began to moan and shout and chant. Bloods who'd stopped going to church and had sworn off the spirit possession of our parents and grandparents began to rock and shake and tremble—yea, they got the Spirit that night! All that college sophistication we had didn't mean a thing! 'Cause Dr. King needed us! The workers down in Mississippi needed us! Our people needed us! Yes sir! We were gonna press on, that night! Ol' Lyndon Johnson, you better listen to us, man! 'Cause we comin'! Marching around your front lawn tonight, buddy! And you're gonna send those troops down to Selma and you're gonna sign that civil rights bill, too! Our time is at hand! This is the new young America talkin' and you'd better listen! Scream, Habiba! Scream, sister! Let us feel those bullets! Let us feel the lash! Scream! Don't let us forget! Bring us home, sister love! Bring us home! Yes sir! Yes, sir! Teach! Teach!

(*Pause*)

We marched in shifts, twenty-four hours a day, seven days. Lyndon Johnson sent the troops and Dr. King made his pilgrimage to Montgomery, where he gave one of the greatest speeches of his life. Still see that speech from time to time on TV. I was listening to it the other day when my oldest son came in and asked me if I could give him some money for new clothes. School was out and they were having a special holiday sale at the mall. Martin Luther King's Birthday.

Talking in Tongues
Winsome Pinnock

A flat in contemporary London. A party. New Year's Eve.

Completely dejected and alone in the midst of a party, Leela, a black woman, sits drinking and crying. Moments before, she came upon her boyfriend, a black man, having sex with the party's hostess, a white woman. Irma, "wearing a multicolored jumpsuit and trainers [sneakers], large gold earrings and . . . a bald head," has been "sitting on the floor in a corner cross-legged," observing Leela's state of misery. "As Leela sobs, [Irma]. . .laughs softly. As Leela's crying gets louder, she can't control her laughter and has to hold her stomach." Leela notices her and stops crying as Irma approaches. Irma "can be played by either a male or female performer." In their brief alcohol-tinged encounter, Irma alludes to a central theme of the play: finding expression for one's innermost emotions. She asks Leela, "Have you never felt the spirit stirring inside you?"

IRMA: You were crying. It always ends in tears. Either that or the china gets broken. (*Pause.*) You don't say much, do you? Not that it matters. I can talk the hind legs off an armchair. (*Pause.*) I was born in south London thirty years ago. My birth was the occasion of great trauma for my mother who, prior to going into labour, had witnessed the strange couplings of common or garden slugs on her kitchen floor at midnight. It wasn't the bizarreness of their copulation that struck her but the realisation that each partner had both projectile and receptacle—she was very fastidious—which, in effect, made the sex act redundant, as a particularly flexible slug could impregnate itself. That such a phenomenon existed on God's earth—she was also very superstitious—undermined the very tenets by which she'd thus far kept her life together. She felt cheated. If God had seen fit to bestow this gift upon human beings then she would not have had to undergo the ritual Friday Night Fuck, a particularly vigorous, not to mention careless, session of which had resulted in my conception. She was overwhelmed by the depth of her anger, and the shock of it propelled her into labour. The doctors didn't know how to tell her at first. It doesn't happen very often, but sometimes a child is born with both receptacle and projectile nestling between its legs. I was such a child and the doctors told my mother that she had to make a choice, or I would be plagued by severe mental confusion and distress for the rest of my life. Of course she didn't know which way to turn. In the end she settled on getting rid of the male appendage, not least because she held the things in contempt but also because she felt that black men were too often in the limelight, and that a woman might quietly get things done while those who undermined her were looking the other way. However, she hadn't reckoned with the fact that she had already become attached to me and found me perfect the way I was. So even while the surgeon was sharpening his knives my mother had wrapped me in an old shawl, woven by her own grandmother, and taken me home. I hope I'm not boring you.

Talk Story
Jeannie Barroga

Act II. Present-day San Francisco. A hotel room.

Frank is the father of Dee, "a Filipina daughter, with a penchant for emu-
lating the heroines of '40s movie flicks, [who] continues her father's legacy
of telling stories to herself and to those around her. She tells her version
of dealing with bigotry much the same way her father told his own heroic
tales to her." Frank is "somewhat itinerant, 70s, a braggart, endearing,
exasperating, lives in a San Francisco hotel," and speaks with a noticeable Filipino accent. He is dressed in "baggy pants, button shirt, hat."
He's been a "lettuce picker . . . cannery worker. . . . Above all, he is a sto-
ryteller." Dee has been grappling with racism (both subtle and overt) in her
job as a journalist and in her relationship with a white colleague. Aspiring
to write a column which tells the stories of Filipino Americans, she tapes her
father's tales from when he was an immigrant to California in the 1930s, a
time when it was illegal for Filipinos to intermarry with Caucasians and
some businesses displayed the sign "NO FILIPINOS ALLOWED."

FRANK: In the Salinas and Central Valleys were jobs for us Pinoys. We
worked alongside the Japanese and the Mexicans. I knew most of
the boys, (*laughs*) the MEN now here in this hotel. By day, in swel-
tering heat like the Islands, we all helped each other. By night, the
Pinoys drove into town to spend the money we had left after sending

most of it to the Islands. Yes, in the fields we were home again, among the green iceberg lettuce and the red leaf lettuce and butter lettuce and brussels sprouts and tomatoes and even the thorny artichokes! Nut-brown hands under the bluest skies and in the darkest soils—just like in the Islands. But the cities beckoned. And I, for one, answered the Call.

When we weren't in the Central Valley in the spring or in the vegetable fields in the summer, we were in the canneries up north in late fall, and hot Southern California every winter. Life was simple, traveling, working, prowling. But then, after awhile, cities were for me.

The more I saw, the more I wanted. The country boy in me was gone. The boy who swam naked in the streams during hot, white Manila days, climbed coconut trees for their sweet, young fruit, washed the month-old piglet in the yard, walked barefoot through pineapple plantations, trailed his brother from place to place—he was gone. . . . (*Strain heard: "Birth of the Blues." [Honky-Tonk version]* PEDRO, *spiffed up, parades as* FRANK *narrates:*) Instead, here was a fresh young man in America: hat-ted, suited, pomaded, perfumed, groomed, BOOTED, shoe-ed, and shod! No more fresh-off-the-boat, no more country bumpkin! I would drink all the liquor and kiss all the girls! I would be sharp and witty and loved. Man-about-town. Twinkling brown eyes, slow, sexy smile. Cigarette between my fingers, brandy on my breath. Gold cuffs, gold tiepin, gold ring, gold watch, gold teeth! (*fantasizes*) Like a . . . a MAYOR! . . .

(PEDRO *exits.*)

But sometimes I miss him, that silly barefoot boy. Cities changed me; now I know only city life in downtown hotels. If you shed enough layers, you won't get them back. Be careful what you let go; be careful what you keep.

Toronto at Dreamer's Rock
Drew Hayden Taylor

Dreamer's Rock, Whitefish River (Birch Island) Reserve, Ontario, Canada.
A lazy Saturday afternoon during the summer of 1989.

Rusty is "a boy from the present," a typical sixteen-year-old teenager,
apathetic about life, flippant, and defensive. He identifies as Indian, half
Odawa and Ojibway, ". . . and I think there's supposed to be some
Pottawatami floating around in my blood somewhere, too." He has come
to Dreamer's Rock, a large outcropping of rock overlooking a scenic valley,
to have a beer. He is "listening to his Walkman, singing a heavy metal tune
at the top of his lungs" when he is startled by a crow and the appearance
of Keesic, "a boy about his age . . . dressed in a buckskin breech, identi-
cal to the kind worn several hundred years ago." Magically they begin to
communicate, although Rusty is certain he is the victim of a practical joke.
When Keesic asks him, ". . . What are you doing on this sacred site? . . . I've
spent the last three days fighting wind and the snow to get here. And only
to be met by summer. Why?" Rusty answers, "Maybe to wear one of those
white jackets with the long arms that wrap right around. . . ." As they
grapple with reality, they are stunned by a newcomer, Michael, "dressed in
unidentifiable futuristic garb." Michael examines them closely and makes
a quick identification, "Pre-contact, no doubt . . . late woodland period"
and "Standard outfitting for the 20th-century aboriginal. Denim. . . ." The
three have been brought together across centuries for some unknown pur-
pose. When Michael and Keesic begin to question Rusty's anger and his

139

beer drinking—"Michael: This particular period of time was known in Aboriginal history as the 'Alcoholic Era. . . .'"—and Keesic speculates, "I don't think you like your life," Rusty explodes in frustration.

Rusty: Do I got a choice? Does it really matter? Okay, I can't go to Hawaii. I'll never own a Porsche, I'll never have all those things I see on television. I'm lucky if I get a new pair of jeans for the first day of school. What's there to be happy for? I'm terrible in school, so I can't walk that side of the tracks, and as for going the traditional Indian route, that's even worse. I hate cleaning fish and I'm a terrible hunter. I don't fit in here. Last year my father took me hunting, I shot my own dog. I can't do anything right except drink. You wanted to know my problems, there they are. I hope you enjoy them.

(*Everybody is silent for a moment, letting the emotion sink in.*)

(Michael: So that's how you deal with your problems. I must say that I'm not particularly impressed. But here. Have another beer! Everybody has problems, but they cope with them.)

Rusty: Oh yeah? Look at you. I have no idea what kind of outfit that is but it don't look like you're too bad off. And judging by the way you talk and the things you've said, you're doing great in school and you know a lot of things. Keesic here only has to worry about hunting enough to eat. They didn't have complicated problems back then. At least you both have your own worlds to fit in and return to. I'm stuck smack-dab in the middle of a family war, between one uncle that's called "Closer" because they say he's closed every bar in Ontario, and my other Uncle Stan, who is basically a powwow Indian, I never know what's going on. Sometimes I don't know if I should go into a sweatlodge or a liquor store. Sometimes they tear me apart. I don't fit in. Like tonight. It's Saturday and what am I doing? Standing on a rock, out in the middle of the woods, talking to two people who probably don't exist. How's that for a social life? Instead of looking at the two of you, I should be out with some hot babe. (*To himself.*) I should have asked her out. I should have.

Weebjob
Diane Glancy

Act 2. Scene 2. The Salazar Canyon in Lincoln County, New Mexico, between Roswell and Socorro.

Gerald Long Chalk, or Weebjob, age 48, is a holy man, a Mescalero Apache. "His name is a play on the Biblical Job because he is beset with problems. . . . He's stern and unyielding, a little impractical, yet likeable. Weebjob always seems to be at a crossroads in his life. He lets rich land lie fallow. He paints signs and hangs them on his fence."

A squash patch with yellow blossoms is where Weebjob communes with Thunder Hawk and where he is found at the start of the play. His best friend, Pick Up, drives up with his daughter, Sweet Potato, after finding her on the highway running away from home. Weebjob's wife, Sweet Grass, has been gone for two weeks without telling Weebjob why she has gone. This scene occurs after Sweet Grass has returned home and Sweet Potato and Pick Up have revealed their love for each other and intention to marry. Weebjob is still reeling from these revelations, ruminating about his three children—"Sweet Potato running off to Gallup. William's unrelenting pursuit of the legal profession, forgetting his spiritual nature. James looking for visions in peyote and drugs. . . ." —as he sits next to his wife Sweet Grass, at her loom. Sweet Potato enters, and their conversation touches upon the difference in her parents' match, when Weebjob went to the Female Seminary looking for a wife, and her own unconventional, intergenerational *love for Pick Up. Weebjob's brief reverie about the Female Seminary leads him to muse about his own boarding school experience and his lifelong hunger for spirituality beyond Christianity.*

WEEBJOB: I remembered when I went to the Female Seminary for a wife. I had a friend who I went to see, and all the girls out on the lawn made me think it was a place to get a wife. I was thinking of the boarding school for Indian boys. . . . (*Pause*) I like this time of evening. I remember the fingers of the sun across the yard of the boarding school from the canyons and arroyos as evening reached from the parched desert. We couldn't ignore it. We woke up in the morning sweating with the heat. It only intensified during the day. We couldn't ignore the poverty of the school. The dreariness of the land. Our heritage was rich with tradition, and it was taken from us. We had to learn a new way, dry and dull, against our reasoning. I longed for Indian ways just as the others. Christianity wasn't enough. And nothing came to fill the particular hunger we felt. Others grew bitter, later drank and wasted their lives. But I have always felt the closeness of the Great Spirit, and that he would manifest himself to me. Why would I have the hunger if there was nothing to fill it? And in the desolation of the nights, when I could hear other boys cry or moan with nightmares, the vision of the Thunder Hawk came, not the vision, for it was the Thunder Hawk himself. A magnificent bird from the spirit world full of light like a blue, stained-glass window in a cathedral. The vine at the window in the winter also reminded me of him. When the land was even deader than it was in summer. The dry vine rattling at the window was like the wings of the Thunder Hawk coming to me right through the walls of the boarding school for Indian boys. It was like the sweat lodge I heard about from the old Indian men before we were taken to school. It seemed to me to be "Canaan" that was talked about in the Book. And this place too, here where I've lived all these years, where I can do what I want without fear or interference. It is "Canaan." I see the Thunder Hawk to this day. He has never left me. Great Spirit, how can you merge with us, who are mortal in our flesh and bound with error and filled with weakness? I must go to the squash patch for a while. I feel the wind over me like the presence of the Great Spirit . . . like the hot shower in the motel in Roswell when William got married and I stayed until the water ran cold and Sweet Grass called for me to get out.

X
Thulani Davis

Act 1. Scene 3. Prison. 1945.

This play begins with the early life of the great black nationalist leader
Malcolm X; we first see Malcolm as "a boy born in terror, marked by our
fear." His father, Reverend Earl Little, wanted to leave America; he
preached the gospel of Marcus Garvey's Back to Africa movement to everyone who would listen. Because of this, he was attacked by a white mob
and lynched by being beaten and left on the streetcar tracks to be run over.
From his father's horrible lynching Malcolm learned that "the cost of freedom is death." Following the killing of her beloved husband, Malcolm's
mother went mad and was unable to care for Malcolm or his three siblings.
They became wards of the state until they could live on their own. As soon
as he came of age, Malcolm left for Boston and joined "the life" filled with
cats, hustlers, zoot suits, conks, and crime. This involvement brought him
to the "wrong side of town," where he robbed "leading citizens" and was
eventually caught and sent to prison. This monologue is his response to a
prison interrogation.

MALCOLM:
I would not tell you
what I know.
You would not

hear my truth.
You want the story
but you don't want to know.
My truth is you've been on me
a very long time,
meaner than I can say.
As long as I've been living
you've had your foot on me,
always pressing.

My truth is white men
killed my old man,
drove my mother mad.
My truth is rough.
My truth could kill.
My truth is fury.

They always told me,
"You don't have a chance.
You're a nigger, after all.
You can jitterbug and prance,
but you'll never run the ball."
My truth told me,
quit before you start.
My truth told me,
stayin' alive is all you've got.

I've shined your shoes,
I've sold your dope,
hauled your bootleg,
played with hustler's hope.

But the crime is mine,
I will do your time,
so you can sleep.
I won't be out to get you
on the street at night
but I won't forget
any evil that's white.

My truth is a hammer
coming from the back.
It will beat you down
when you least expect.
I would not tell you
what I know.
You want the truth,
you want the truth,
but you don't want to know.

(*Lights out.*)

Yankee Dawg You Die
Philip Kan Gotanda

Act 2, Scene 1. An Acting Class.

Bradley Yamashita is a Japanese American actor in his mid-to late twenties. At a party in the Hollywood Hills he meets Vincent Chang, a youthful, silver-maned, sixtyish Chinese American actor who has established himself in the motion picture industry. Bradley is eager to meet Vincent: "Everybody knows who you are. Especially in the community. . . ." Vincent, on the other hand is nonplused: "I do not really notice, or quite frankly care, if someone is Caucasian or oriental. . . ." Thus begins an uneasy relationship, as they intersect at auditions and acting class. Bradley is the brash, ambitious upstart, and Vincent is the pro who has smashed the barriers, giving Bradley greater opportunities. Although generationally and culturally at odds, Vincent recognizes Bradley's tenacity and talent. Together in an acting class, he leads Bradley in a method-acting exercise: "Become a . . . rock. You are a rock. Find your shape. Are you big, small, flat, oblong? Keep looking until you find your own particular shape." Becoming a rock, Bradley relives an acid trip he once took.

Bradley: I have been a rock before. . . . I have. On acid. LSD. The first time I dropped acid I walked into a forest in the Santa Cruz mountains and became a rock. . . . I was in college. . . . (*Suppressing giggle*) I am walking. There is a tightness I feel in the back of my neck—I guess it's the acid coming on. With each step I go deeper into the forest. And with each step I can feel the civilized part of me peeling away like an old skin. Whoa, my mind is beginning to cast aside whole concepts. God, the earth is breathing. I can feel it. It's like standing on someone's tummy. And this rock. This big, beautiful rock. Our consciousnesses are very similar. I do a Vulcan mind-meld. (*Touching the rock*) "I am waiting for nothing. I am expecting no one." (*Releases Vulcan mind-meld*) It is beautiful in its own rock-ness. . . . I begin walking again. . . . Thoughts of great insight float in and out of my mind like pretty butterflies. Skin holds the body together. But what holds the mind together? *What holds the mind together?* I panic! I feel my mind beginning to drift away. There is nothing to hold my mind together. Soon bits and pieces of my con-sciousness will be scattered across the universe. I'll NEVER GRAD-UATE! What? What's this? Cows. Ten, twenty, sixty, hundreds. Hundreds and hundreds of cows. Where did they come from? They spot me. They see that I am different. One cow steps forward. She is the leader. She wears a bell as a sign of her authority. She approaches me cautiously, studying me. The head cow nods in approval. She knows I am no longer a civilized human, but some-how different, like them. She turns and signals the others. They all begin to move toward me. Soon I am surrounded in a sea of friendly cows. Hello, hi—it's like old home week. Suddenly I hear a noise coming from far away. It tugs at something inside me. I turn to see where the noise is coming from. I see . . . I recognize . . . Jeffrey. My best friend. Calling my name. I look at the cows. They are waiting to see what I will do. I look at Jeffrey, his voice ringing clearer and clearer, my name sounding more and more familiar. I look at the cows—they are beginning to turn away. Should I stay and run wild and free with the cows? Or should I return to the dorms on campus? "HOWDY, JEFFREY!" As I look back, the cows are once again pre-tending to be cows. They slowly lumber away, stupid and dumb. Moo, moo. (BRADLEY *notices* VINCENT *staring at him.*) It's a true story.

Zooman and the Sign
Charles Fuller

Act 1. Scene 1.

Zooman is "a young black man who addresses the world "contemptuously."
He wears a T-shirt "with the inscription 'Me' on it . . . hightop sneakers . . .
and several thin gold and silver chains around his neck." He crosses
onstage "with a stylized dancewalk 'bobbing' movement." This play is
about Zooman and the black family whose young daughter he killed in an
act of random and senseless violence.

ZOOMAN: Once upon a time, while the goose was drinkin' wine? Ole'
monkey robbed the people on the trolley car line. (*Laughs.*) I carry
a gun and a knife. A gun in this pocket—and ole' "Magic" in this
one! (*Takes out knife and flicks it open.*) Now you see it—(*makes a
stabbing gesture*) Now you don't! (*Smiles.*) I cut a mothafucka' with
this baby yesterday. Ole' foreigner walking on the subway platform.
(*He waddles, amused.*) Arms swingin' all ova' everywhere—bumpin'
into people—glasses, two, three inches thick standin' out from his
eyes, can't half see! And I'm trying to listen to my music too? No-
talking mothafucka' needed to get cut. (*Smiles.*) Magic nicked him.
Magic is sharp as a razor. He ain't even know he was cut 'til he was
halfway down the platform, and the blood started runnin' down the

153

ole' punk's hand. (*Looks at the knife.*) Mothafucka' started screamin'—dropped his newspapa'—jumpin' up and down, pleadin' to everybody waitin' on the subway. Ain' nobody do nothin'—ole' jive West Indian mothafucka' damn near got hit by a train! (*Laughs.*) Fell all down on the ground and shit—peed on hisself! Shiiit, he wasn't hurt that bad! Magic only nicked the scared mothafucka'! (*To himself, after a pause:*) Mothafucka' don't know what scared is! (*Crosses onto the sidewalk area; distinct change of mood.*) They call me, Zooman! That's right. Z-O-O-M-A-N! From the Bottom! I'm the runner down thea'. When I knuck with a dude, I fight like a panther. Strike like a cobra! Stomp on mothafuckas' like a whole herd of bi-son! Zooman! (*Irritated.*) That ole' mothafucka' yesterday coulda' put somebody's eye out. Swinging his arms around like he owned the whole fuckin' platform. Lotta' ole' people take advantage of you jes' cause they ole'. Movin' all slow and shit—mumblin' unda' they breath—(*crosses onto his platform*) shufflin' down the street all bent ova and twisted up—skin hangin' off they faces—makes my stomach turn jes' to look at 'em! I got an aunt like that. Me and Kenny useta' stay to that mean bitch's house sometimes. Evil ole' skunk walkin' down the avenue, one mile an hour and shit, useta hit us across the mouth with a fly swatter jes' for talkin' at the mothafuckin' table! I was glad when the junkies would steal her check. We useta' tell her, she was dumb for goin' down there—don't nobody with any sense walk on the Avenue with a social-security check in they hands! (*To himself:*) Lotta' times we'd be to that bitch's house, three—four days, wouldn't eat nothin'. (*Casually crosses onto sidewalk.*) What am I doing here now? I just killed somebody. Little girl, I think. Me and Stockholm turned the corner of this street—and there's Gustav and them jive mothafuckas' from uptown, and this litte bitch has to be sitting on her front steps playing jacks—or some ole' kid shit! But I had tol' Gustav if I eva' saw his ass around the Avenue, I'd blow him away. (*Shrugs.*) So I started shootin' and she jes' got hit by one of the strays, that's all. She ain't had no business bein' out there. That street is a war zone—ain' nobody see her, we was runnin'—shit! And in that neighborhood you supposed to stay indoors, anyway! (*Pause.*) She was in the wrong place at the wrong time—how am I supposed to feel guilty over somethin' like that? Shiiit, I don't know the little bitch, anyway. (ZOOMAN *exits.*)

Acknowledgments

The editor wishes to acknowledge and thank New WORLD Theater staff: BRANDON ANDERSON, LUCY MAE, SAN PABLO BURNS, JESUS MACLEAN, JOE SALVATORE, JESSICA SHADOIAN, SUSANNE MUSSMANN, ANGEL HARDY and JEN WERNER for assistance with research and DENNIS CONWAY, YVONNE MENDEZ, LISA HORI-GARCIA, KARIMA ROBINSON, MARY MURATORE, and JAVIERA BENAVENTE for keeping the theater going strong during this project. Special thanks to FRED TILLIS and LEE EDWARDS for their mentorship, and to LEN BERKMAN, SHELBY JIGGETTS-TIVONY, RICHARD TROUSDELL, HARLEY ERDMAN, and BETSY THEOBALD for their sound advice. For their love, patience and support, thank-you to my children and husband: CHINUA AKIMARO THELWELL, MIKIKO AKEMI THELWELL, and ANDREW CONDRON.

Permissions and Play Sources

obtaining in advance, the written permission of the Dramatists Play Service, Inc., and paying the requisite fee. Inquiries regarding all other rights should be addressed to Gilbert Parker, William Morris Agency, Inc., 1325 Avenue of the Americas, New York, NY 10019. **DEATH AND THE MAIDEN** by Ariel Dorfman (Penguin, 1991). © 1992, Ariel Dorfman. Used by permission of Viking Penguin, a division of Penguin Putnam, Inc. **DRY LIPS OUGHTA MOVE TO KAPUSKASING** by Tomson Highway (Fifth House, 1989). Copyright © 1989 by Tomson Highway. Reprinted by permission of Fifth House, Ltd., Calgary, Alberta, Canada. **DUTCHMAN** by LeRoi Jones (Amiri Baraka) appears in *Contemporary Black Drama*, edited by Clinton F. Oliver and Stephanie Sils (Charles Scribner's Sons, 1971). Copyright © 1964 by Amiri Baraka. Reprinted by permission of Sterling Lord Literistic, Inc. **EDUCATION IS OUR RIGHT** by Drew Hayden Taylor appears in *Dreamer's Rock: Two One Act Plays* by Drew Hayden Taylor (Fifth House, 1990). Copyright © 1990 by Drew Hayden Taylor. Reprinted by permission of Fifth House Ltd., Calgary, Alberta, Canada. **EL GRITO DE LAS MINAS** by Anthony J. Garcia appears in *Su Teatro 20 Year Anthology* (Su Teatro Publications). **FIERCE LOVE** by Pomo Afro Homos appears in *Colored Contradictions*, edited by Harry J. Elam, Jr. and Robert Alexander (Plume, 1996). **FIRES IN THE MIRROR** by Anna Deavere Smith (Anchor Books, 1993). Reprinted by permission of Anna Deavere Smith and the Watkins/Loomis Agency. **THE FIRST BREEZE OF SUMMER** by Leslie Lee appears in *Black Thunder*, edited by William Branch (Mentor, 1992). Reprinted by permission of Samuel French, Inc. **FISH HEAD SOUP** by Philip Kan Gotanda appears in *Fish Head Soup and Other Plays* by Philip Kan Gotanda (University of Washington Press, 1991). Reprinted by permission of the Joyce Ketay Agency. **FOR BLACK BOYS WHO HAVE CONSIDERED HOMICIDE WHEN THE STREETS WERE TOO MUCH** by Keith Antar Mason appears in *Colored Contradictions*, edited by Harry J. Elam, Jr. and Robert Alexander (Plume, 1996). Reprinted by permission of the author. **49** by Hanay Geiogamah appears in *New Native American Drama* (University of Oklahoma Press, 1980). Copyright © 1980 by the University of Oklahoma, Norman. Reprinted by permission of the University of Oklahoma Press. **THE GATE OF HEAVEN** by Lane Nishikawa and Victor Talmadge appears in *Asian American Drama*, edited by Brian Nelson (Applause, 1997). **I AM A MAN** by OyamO appears courtesy of the author. **I HATE** by Bernardo Solano appears courtesy of the author. **A JAMAICAN AIRMAN FORESEES HIS OWN DEATH** by Fred D'Aguiar appears in *Black Plays: Three* (Methuen, 1995). Reprinted by permission of the Curtis Brown Group. **JOE TURNER'S COME AND GONE** by August Wilson (Plume 1988). Copyright © 1988 by August Wilson. Used by permission of Dutton Signet, a division of Penguin Putnam Inc. **A LANGUAGE OF THEIR OWN** by Chay Yew appears in *But Still Like Air I'll Rise*, edited by Velina Hasu Houston (Temple University Press, 1997). Reprinted by permission of Grove/Atlantic, Inc. **LATINS ANONYMOUS** by Latins Anonymous appears in *Latins Anonymous—Two Plays* by Latins Anonymous (Arte Público Press, 1996). Reprinted by permission of Arte Público Press. **THE LION AND THE JEWEL** by Wole Soyinka appears in *Wole Soyinka: Collected Plays 2* (Oxford University Press, 1974). Reprinted by permission of Oxford University Press. **MA RAINEY'S BLACK BOTTOM** by August Wilson appears in *Totem Voices*, edited by Paul Carter Harrison (Grove, 1989). Copyright © 1985 by August Wilson. Used by permission of Dutton Signet, a division of Penguin Putnam Inc. **THE MEETING** by Jeff Stetson appears in *The National Black Drama Anthology* (Applause Books, 1995). Reprinted by permission of the author. **MEN ON THE VERGE OF A HIS-PANIC BREAKDOWN** by Guillermo Reyes appears in *Staging Gay Lives*, edited by John M. Clum (Westview, 1996). Reprinted by permission of the author. **THE MIGHTY GENTS** by Richard Wesley (Dramatists Play Service, 1979). **MIRIAM'S FLOWERS** by Migdalia Cruz appears in *Shattering*